Brian Zahnd is blunt, bold, and biblical: we simply cannot embrace violence and retaliation in the name of Jesus. As he juxtaposes the centrality of the cross of Jesus ("Father, forgive them") and the teaching of Jesus ("love your enemies"), he exposes the blasphemous absurdity of hating our enemies in Jesus's name. An authentic prophetic voice in the lineage of Elijah and Amos.

—EUGENE H. PETERSON
PROFESSOR EMERITUS OF SPIRITUAL THEOLOGY
REGENT COLLEGE, VANCOUVER, BC

What a book! This book, *Radical Forgiveness*, by Brian Zahnd, is the best I have ever read on the subject of forgiveness. It is a riveting and challenging book. But above all, it calls Christians to a deeper understanding of how liberating true forgiveness can be and how the church could be transformed by the principles set forth in this excellent book, which could become a classic.

—VINSON SYNAN
PROFESSOR OF CHURCH HISTORY AND DEAN EMERITUS
REGENT UNIVERSITY

What pastor and author Brian Zahnd has to say to the evangelical church in *Radical Forgiveness* is nothing short of prophetic. His message of returning to the practice of radical forgiveness provides new perspectives and guidance to Christians as we attempt to move forward in a culture where "The Bible says so" has become an ineffective response to the questions and issues of today's unchurched. Zahnd brings us back to the cross of the One we follow, reminding us that forgiving love will be the one effective platform for the church as we seek to engage others in the gospel.

—LINDY LOWRY
EDITOR, *OUTREACH MAGAZINE*

Relentlessly biblical, theologically pure, pastorally tested. Brian challenges the church to become Christian. He proclaims the centrality of forgiving love in Christ's invitation such that we might just hesitate before entering that narrow gate. This message might actually save us.

—BRAD JERSAK
AUTHOR OF *CAN YOU HEAR ME?*

Hannah Arendt (probably one of the finest political philosophers of the twentieth century) suggested, in her classic tome *The Human Condition*, that the notion of forgiveness was one of the most significant contributions Christianity has made to the world. Arendt, as a Jew, knew of what she spoke. Brian Zahnd's *Radical Forgiveness* amply illustrates why forgiveness is the heartbeat and core of an authentic and costly grace-filled life. Do meditatively read and inwardly digest this gem and jewel of a classic in the making. Your faith journey will be transformed into pure gold.

—RON DART
DEPARTMENT OF POLITICAL SCIENCE/PHILOSOPHY/
RELIGIOUS STUDIES
UNIVERSITY OF THE FRASER VALLEY
ABBOTSFORD, BRITISH COLUMBIA, CANADA

In *Radical Forgiveness* Brian Zahnd calls us to the table of the Lord, where forgiveness is the main course! There's a table calling me home, to look in the eyes of a friend and forget they were my enemy, and see the way that I can be.

—JASON UPTON
RECORDING ARTIST

Pastor Brian Zahnd is a fellow dreamer with a daring vision for the church today. He is a passionate voice offering practical and biblical revelation on the art of forgiveness and the challenge of following Christ's example in our everyday lives. The call to radical forgiveness is one we must all answer, just as Jesus did through his unselfish, unconditional, and radical death on the cross.

—BRIAN HOUSTON
SENIOR PASTOR, HILLSONG CHURCH

Utterly compelling reading.

—R. T. KENDALL
BEST-SELLING AUTHOR OF *TOTAL FORGIVENESS*

As a pastor, I have read many excellent books on forgiveness. Brian Zahnd's is among the finest I've ever read. This book is filled with inspiring stories of forgiveness and keen theological and biblical insights. If I had to recommend just one book on forgiveness, this would be it.

—Rev. Adam Hamilton
Senior Pastor, Church of the Resurrection
Author of *When Christians Get It Wrong*

In a world filled with animosity and hostility, Brian Zahnd challenges readers to rediscover the heart of the Christian gospel—a revolution of forgiving love. *Radical Forgiveness* is a welcomed change to the worn-out rhetoric and dead-end discussions concerning how we can overcome conflict and hurt. Zahnd's thoughtful vision of forgiveness is biblical, beautiful, brilliant, and bold. He gives us the way forward by framing the need for interpersonal forgiveness with historical and contemporary stories of atrocity, brutality, war, and suffering. Along the way he interacts with thinkers, writers, poets, statesmen, philosophers, and theologians in producing a masterful appeal for followers of Christ to "end the cycle of revenge." *Radical Forgiveness* is not a safe book. It is a dangerous call to take seriously the biblical command to forgive one another.

—Dr. Derek Vreeland
Pastor, Cornerstone Church, Americus, Georgia
Author of *Shape Shifters: How God
Changes the Human Heart*

I love this book! This is not a glib treatment of forgiveness. It begins with the Holocaust and proceeds from there. This is about deep, costly forgiveness. It deals with the heart of the Christian faith: the grand announcement of good news, the best news of all, the unconditional, radical forgiveness of sin by Christ's sacrificial life, death, and all-encompassing, victorious resurrection.

—Joe Beach
Amazing Grace Church, Denver, CO

Brian Zahnd has issued a much-needed call to every one of us to better understand and live out the implications of the cross— forgiveness. Written from the heart of a pastor and the keen mind of a reformer, this book will both challenge and inspire you.

—Lee Cummings
Pastor, Radiant Church, Richland, MI

I love this book. Radical forgiveness is the most important—and most difficult—ethical imperative there is. Ultimately it's what we mean when we talk about unconditional love, if that love is going to be put to the test. Most people want to offer love that is weightless. This book couldn't be more important. It is also very gracefully written. Zahnd's voice—a very compelling voice—is 100 percent there, nothing fake, nothing contrived. People will love the book if they read it. I very much hope they do.

—CLANCY MARTIN
PROFESSOR OF PHILOSOPHY
UNIVERSITY OF MISSOURI–KANSAS CITY

Radical Forgiveness should be required reading for all to understand the concept of unconditional love and forgiveness. As the niece of a Holocaust survivor, I have often asked myself the very question posed by this book—"What would I have done?" Zahnd challenges us, more so as Christians, to take forgiveness to an unprecedented level and to truly forgive as Jesus did. Eye opening, thought provoking; a must-read!

—DR. SHERILL PISCOPO
EVANGEL ASSOCIATION OF CHURCHES & MINISTRIES
ROSEVILLE, MI

Brian Zahnd has done it again! His first book was incredible, but *Radical Forgiveness* marks him as a writer always worth reading. In a world filled with surface answers, Brian gives real unvarnished truth. We all struggle to integrate the teachings of Jesus into our everyday lives. Pastor Zahnd confronts, challenges, and motivates us all to the radical claims of Jesus. One of the best books on forgiveness that I have ever read. Thank you!

—MICHAEL S. STEWART
PRESIDENT, EMMANUEL COLLEGE,
FRANKLIN SPRINGS, GA

Radical Forgiveness would have to be one of the most profound books that I have read for a few years. With most books you read them. I think that this book reads you, engages with your mind, challenges your spirit, and at times lays bare your soul and emotions—while offering the remedy in Christ. I trust that it finds itself into the hands of many, not for the sales it can make, but for the lives it can change.

—RUSSELL DUNN
GENERAL MANAGER, MANNA CHRISTIAN STORES
AUCKLAND, NEW ZEALAND

Radical Forgiveness graciously challenges both the mind and spirit with the Christ follower's personal responsibility to break the revenge cycle and forgive others regardless of the offense. Zahnd clearly communicates this Christian distinctive for radical forgiveness with the Word of God, powerfully illustrated by contemporary as well as historic examples. I read a lot of books. This one spoke deeply to my heart.

—DR. BILL JONES
PRESIDENT, COLUMBIA INTERNATIONAL UNIVERSITY

In his book *Radical Forgiveness*, Brian Zahnd offers a powerful portrayal of the beauty of love and forgiveness that answer the question of whether anything is too hateful or painful to forgive. As Zahnd states it, "We live in a world where much is wrong." But in this book he inspires belief in the "radical proposition that love is more powerful than hate" and reminds us that forgiveness can indeed be radical through the example and extension of grace through Jesus Christ.

—MINISTER JUDY JACOBS TUTTLE
HIS SONG MINISTRIES

Wow! A vital avenue toward the road of healing and living life uninhibited! Pastor Zahnd has managed to capture sincere, real, and revoluntionary truths and convey them in a practical, authentic, yet convicting expression. This information is much needed in such a hurting and ailing society. *Radical Forgiveness* motivates one to devote radical application of its information because of the revelation of God's unfailing faithfulness in our journey through this life.

—JOEL E. GREGORY
SENIOR PASTOR, FAITH CHRISTIAN CENTER
SMYRNA, GA

Forgiveness takes on a whole new meaning in this powerful book, because forgiveness for the Christian is really radical—just as Jesus intended it to be. Brian Zahnd takes the reader on a journey that at times is breathtaking. He reminds us that forgiveness is one of the most difficult acts in all of our lives, yet he fully explains how we can radically forgive and become a living imitation of Jesus Christ. His illustrations and true stories of forgiveness are unimaginable yet real, leaving you with the realization that you want to be that type of forgiving Christian.

—JON R. WALLACE, DBA
PRESIDENT, AZUSA PACIFIC UNIVERSITY

Many books have been written on forgiveness, but *Radical Forgiveness* marks a fresh and useful approach to this vital subject. Its pages are loaded with insights on how radical forgiveness can reverse the toxic cycle of bitterness and revenge for individuals, families—even nations. *Radical Forgiveness* will convict you of the devastating results of pursuing vengeance under the guise of justice and convince you of the value of the alternative—Christ's way of forgiveness.

—DON HAWKINS, DMIN
PRESIDENT, SOUTHEASTERN BIBLE COLLEGE
BIRMINGHAM, AL

Heads up! Pay close attention to this author. The message of *Radical Forgiveness* is a timely and much needed reminder of what is central to the gospel—a truth both beautiful and good and more desired by secular seekers and discouraged disciples than many of us realize. The author's personal and pastoral journey is itself an equally powerful bit of encouragement for all of us in ministry and mission who find ourselves in luminal space. Brian Zahnd is a master storyteller with the intellectual horsepower of a Miroslav Volf, the pastoral heart and credible record of effective congregational leadership of a John Ortberg, and a capacity for articulating the gospel across generations and tribes on a par with Eugene Peterson. Here is an evangelical colleague to whom leaders in mainline and Catholic circles are listening with great interest.

—BILL ROSE-HEIM
NW AREA PASTOR
CHRISTIAN CHURCH (DISCIPLES OF CHRIST) IN MID-AMERICA

Radical
FORGIVENESS

BRIAN ZAHND

PASSIO

Cover design by Lisa Rae Cox
Design Director: Bill Johnson

Visit the author's website at www.brianzahnd.com.

Library of Congress Control Number: 2012955814
International Standard Book Number: 978-1-62136-252-4
E-book ISBN: 978-1-62136-526-6

While the author has made every effort to provide accurate telephone numbers and Internet addresses at the time of publication, neither the publisher nor the author assumes any responsibility for errors or for changes that occur after publication.

Previously published as *Unconditional?* by Charisma House, ISBN 978-1-61638-025-0, copyright © 2010.

13 14 15 16 17 — 9 8 7 6 5 4 3 2 1
Printed in the United States of America

For Peri...

*My constant companion in the
adventure of faith*

CONTENTS

FOREWORD

I HAVE BEEN WAITING for a book like the one you are holding in your hand.

I grew up a son of a Pentecostal minister. God found the way into my father's heart in a hell of a Communist concentration camp. From a raging atheist he became a follower of Christ. He survived—barely—and joined a small Pentecostal church in the former Yugoslavia. He fasted for weeks to receive the baptism in the Spirit. He spoke in tongues, he had a gift of interpretation, and he practiced laying on of hands and praying for the sick. For two weeks in 1958, during a visit to the United States, he went to Tulsa, Oklahoma, and was taught by Oral Roberts.

After my own brief stint as a "prodigal," I was baptized in his church and became a committed Pentecostal. It is there that I preached my first sermon, and it is there that I made my first steps in leading the people of God. He had hoped that I would succeed him as the pastor of that church. It is also in my father's orbit that I wrote my first theological texts and undertook the translation of Christian books. (As a teenager, I translated John Sherrill's book *They Speak With Other Tongues* into Croatian, a sympathetic report of an encounter with Pentecostalism.) As a young man, I was an active Pentecostal, but that began to change after I arrived in California in the fall of 1977 and encountered American Pentecostalism.

I went to study theology at Fuller Theological Seminary, not too far from Azusa Street in Los Angeles, the place where the original Pentecostal flame was lit. The Maye family—people as good as any I had met anywhere—gave me, a stranger, their TV room as my new home. As I flipped through the channels one evening, I stumbled upon an over-the-top flamboyant TV evangelist, who was, among other bizarre things, pulling evil spirits out of people's ears. I was shocked not so much by the strange spectacle as by what seemed to me a complete lack of spiritual depth. Soon I found that he was not alone. On television and in many churches, preachers were peddling a compromised gospel of health, wealth, and power, which believers had a right to claim as their own by a simple act of faith. That seemed to me a faith designed not to direct peoples' striving toward God and neighbor, but to feed the black hole of their self-absorption and greed.

When Pentecostalism came of age and gained some respectability, the vision of the healing of bodies expanded to include the goal of healing the nation. And yet the causes many Pentecostals took on were often driven less by the gospel of God's care for all than by concern for ourselves, our material well-being, and our security. Until recently, many Pentecostals supported environmental policies that consisted mainly in making sure that God's creation remains as unprotected from human rapaciousness as possible. This was a very shortsighted policy, even if one thinks only of human interests. The worst of it is that it was meant to be shortsighted. For soon the Terrible Day of the Lord would come, many believed, and the whole earth with all its resources would be swallowed up in one massive conflagration. So, they reasoned, we better rescue as much of it to our use as possible before it all goes up in smoke! Again, wealth and power were almost the exclusive concern.

And then came the "war against terror" and the obsession with security. After 9/11, America was gripped by the spirit of the "kick-butt" culture (to use a phrase from Zahnd's book). Many Pentecostals, along with many evangelicals, believed that the war was really a face-off between the Yahweh of the Bible and Allah, the moon god of the Quran. Soon after I arrived in the United States, I came to realize that American Pentecostals are among the most enthusiastic warriors in the culture wars and eager proponents of an aggressive foreign policy especially unkind to the enemies of freedom, whether these are Communists or Muslims.

This was not the Pentecostal faith of the Azusa Street Revival, of the band of those who gathered around William Joseph Seymour and of the first generation of Pentecostals. And this was not the Pentecostal faith I learned from my father—a Christian with deep spiritual sensitivities and a man who was gripped by God's love in the depth of his own misery. He believed that God lifted people out of poverty, but he was persuaded God does so primarily through people who are willing to give and work for the poor and disadvantaged. At our kitchen table, he never prayed that God would "shower blessings" on the poor, but that God would open our hands to be generous to them. He believed that people had the right to use the rich resources of God's creation. It would have never occurred to him, however, that this gave humans license to pillage and destroy what God has declared as good. As for enemies, he taught me that Christ died for the ungodly, as the apostle Paul says. And he reminded me more than once that during his earthly sojourn Jesus commanded his followers to love their neighbors, including their enemies. In his old age, he insisted that an Albanian Muslim, for whom he worked as a young confectioner, was "the best man for whom I have ever worked."

My father's Pentecostal faith and American Pentecostalism clashed in my experience. I felt a deep discomfort with American Pentecostalism. I knew, of course, that there was much more to it than the health and wealth "gospel," disregard for God's creation, and an aggressive policy toward all enemies, domestic and foreign. My friends like William W. Menzies (who befriended me when I was a teenager hungry for theological learning), Cecil M. Robeck (with whom I taught at Fuller Theological Seminary), Joseph Cumming (who works on reconciliation between Muslims and Christians at the Center that I direct at Yale), and many other American Pentecostals embody this alternative. And yet what I saw in many churches and on television seemed so acquisitive and aggressive, so self-absorbed and unforgiving that I could recognize in it neither the faith of my father nor the faith of Jesus's followers.

Now you know why I've been waiting for a book like Brian Zahnd's *Radical Forgiveness*. In a fresh and compelling way, Zahnd urges all of us to give up on consumerism and hostility toward those who differ from us and practice generous and forgiving grace. His book is an urgent summons to conversion. It is an echo of the call that comes from the deepest abyss of God's heart—the call to find our deepest joy by becoming instruments of God's unconditional love. My father is smiling from heaven. And maybe William Seymour is too.

—MIROSLAV VOLF

Miroslav Volf is Henry B. Wright Professor of Theology at Yale University and Founding Director of the Yale Center for Faith and Culture. He is author of *Exclusion and Embrace* (Abingdon) and *Free of Charge: Giving and Forgiving in a Culture Stripped of Grace* (Zondervan).

PRELUDE

ESTERN CHRISTIANITY IS in need of an update. I would go so far as to say the need is desperate. Christianity, by which I mean the experience of living the message of Jesus, should always be characterized by a compelling freshness and vibrancy. But what passes for the Christian message today feels a bit old and tired. I fear that Christianity as it is presently understood is in danger of fading into a kind of cherished relic. It has happened before. If Christianity is to be a compelling and relevant voice in the twenty-first century, it needs a fresh message—not a new innovation or novel interpretation, but a return to our roots. And what are our roots? To a certain extent that is what this book is about.

The primary experience and central emphasis of Christianity revolves around the theme of forgiveness. If Christianity is about anything, it is about forgiveness. Not forgiveness as merely an end in itself or a legal means of escaping punishment, but forgiveness as reconciliation and total restoration. Christianity presents forgiveness as the restoration of the troubled relationship between God and humanity. Forgiveness is also that which alone has the capacity to achieve peace and reconciliation within human relationships—whether personal or global. Most importantly this is a book about how Jesus forgives and how he calls us to imitate his practice of radical forgiveness. And *radical* is the appropriate word, because when it comes to the proclamation and practice of forgiveness, Jesus was the most radical innovator in history. When Jesus teaches on forgiveness, he pushes us into the extreme. Jesus seems to be indicating that our practice of forgiveness should be unconditional. But unconditional forgiveness is a tall order, and it requires some serious thought. Can we always forgive? Should we always forgive? If we always forgive, aren't we enabling evil? If we forgive unconditionally, aren't we sacrificing justice? These are some of the issues I attempt to explore in this book.

> *If Christianity is about anything,*
> *it is about forgiveness.*

While writing I have primarily had a Christian audience in mind, as I assume Christians will comprise the majority of my readers. But to those who do not identify themselves as Christians, I want to say I have also kept you in mind. I invite you to regard this book as my summation of what I think Christianity in its essence is all about. And to the critic of Christianity, I would like to acknowledge that I am sadly aware that at times Christianity has not been very pretty. Too often the message of Jesus has been misrepresented by the ugly faces of legalism, triumphalism, and religiously inspired hatred. (I address some of these issues in the book.) My hope is that you will allow me to present to you the beautiful face of Christianity—the face of forgiveness.

Perhaps this has been my primary motive in writing this book—to help recover the true beauty of Christianity as found in forgiveness. As we enter the second decade of the third Christian millennium, we are a church in need of a renovation—a renovation that I'm convinced can be achieved by a recovery of the beautiful Christian gospel of forgiveness. In a world where the ugliness of rage and retaliation are driving the story line of the twenty-first century, the beauty of authentic Christian forgiveness is the compelling alternative.

—BRIAN ZAHND

*Forgive us our trespasses as we forgive
those who trespass against us.*
JESUS, FROM THE LORD'S PRAYER

❖〰❖

Father, forgive them.
JESUS, AS HE HUNG UPON THE CROSS

❖〰❖

If you forgive the sins of any, they are forgiven.
JESUS, IN HIS FIRST POST-RESURRECTION
APPEARANCE TO HIS APOSTLES

❖〰❖

I believe in the forgiveness of sins.
THE APOSTLES' CREED

1

THE QUESTION OF FORGIVENESS

I T SHOULD BE obvious that forgiveness lies at the heart of the Christian faith, for at its most crucial moments the gracious melody of forgiveness is heard as the recurring theme of Christianity. Consider the prevalence of forgiveness in Christianity's moments of birth and sacred texts: As Jesus teaches his disciples to pray, they are instructed to say, "Forgive us our sins, for we ourselves forgive everyone who is indebted to us."* As Jesus hangs upon the cross, we hear him pray—almost unbelievably—"Father, forgive them."† In his first resurrection appearance to his disciples, Jesus says, "If you forgive the sins of any, they are forgiven."‡ In the Apostles' Creed we are taught to confess, "I believe in the forgiveness of sins."

Whether we look to the Lord's Prayer or Jesus's death upon the cross or his resurrection or the great creeds of the church, we are never far from the theme of forgiveness—for if Christianity isn't about forgiveness, it's about nothing at all. Whatever

---

* Luke 11:4
† Luke 23:34
‡ John 20:23

1

else may be said about Christian people, it must be said of us that we are a people who believe in the forgiveness of sins—we believe in the forgiveness of sins as surely as we believe in the death and resurrection of Jesus Christ. Most of us enter the Christian faith at least somewhat motivated, if not primarily motivated, to find forgiveness for our own sins. As we grow in the Christian faith, it is vital we become aware that we are called to be those who extend forgiveness to others, thus making the world a more forgiving place. If we enter the Christian faith to find forgiveness, we must continue in the faith to become forgiving people, because to be an authentic follower of Christ we must embrace the centrality of forgiveness.

> *If Christianity isn't about forgiveness,*
> *it's about nothing at all.*

That's the theory anyway.

But in the real world of murder, rape, child abuse, genocide, and horrible atrocities, how viable is forgiveness? Is forgiveness just a pious idea that can flourish inside stained-glass sanctuaries, only to wither in the harsh realities of a secular world where stained glass cannot hide the ugliness of human atrocity? A rape victim may have learned the Lord's Prayer as a child in Sunday school, but does the part about forgiving those who trespass against us have any bearing upon her situation? Is she supposed to forgive her rapist? Sure, forgiveness is good in the realm of relatively minor transgressions, but is there a limit to forgiveness? Are there some crimes that go beyond the capacity of forgiveness? Are there some sins so heinous that to forgive them would itself be an immoral act? Is forgiveness always possible? Or even always right? These are not theoretical questions; these are real questions that are forced upon us in a world where evil is so often beyond the pale.

For modern people, the iconic image of evil and the leading candidate for the unforgivable is the Holocaust and the evil architect of that atrocity, Adolf Hitler. Indeed, the Holocaust casts a long shadow over many aspects of the Christian faith and challenges Christian validity on several levels. While considering the topic of forgiveness, we must ask: Does the Christian concept of forgiveness have anything to do with the Holocaust, or is genocide indeed the realm of the unforgivable? When Christianity speaks of forgiveness, should there be an asterisk attached to the word to indicate that forgiveness is not applicable in extreme situations like the concentration camps of Nazi Germany, the ethnic cleansing in the former Yugoslavia, and the tribal massacres of Rwanda?

I've had people tell me not to worry about these extreme cases, because to teach people to forgive one another in the ordinary course of life is enough. But I disagree. If it can be shown that there are situations in which the call of Christ to love our enemies and forgive our transgressors does not apply, we have found the loophole to escape any meaningful Christian obligation to forgive others. Forgiveness then indeed becomes merely an ideal of piety restricted to a stained-glass showcase. The questions about how far forgiveness can and should extend are real questions asked by real people—perhaps most notably by Simon Wiesenthal.

"What I Am Asking Is Almost Too Much"

Simon Wiesenthal has a haunting story to tell, and an even more haunting question to ask. He tells his story and asks his question in his famous book *The Sunflower*. Simon Wiesenthal was an Austrian Jew imprisoned in a Nazi concentration camp during World War II. In *The Sunflower*, Simon Wiesenthal tells his story and then asks the reader a hard question.

As the book opens, Wiesenthal is part of a work detail being taken from the concentration camp to do cleanup work in a makeshift field hospital near the Eastern Front. As they are marched from the prison camp to the hospital, they come across a cemetery for German soldiers. On each grave is a sunflower. Wiesenthal writes:

> I envied the dead soldiers. Each had a sunflower to connect him with the living world, and butterflies to visit his grave. For me there would be no sunflower. I would be buried in a mass grave, where corpses would be piled on top of me. No sunflower would ever bring light into my darkness, and no butterflies would dance above my dreadful tomb.[1]

While working at the field hospital, a German nurse orders Wiesenthal to follow her. He is taken into a room where a lone SS soldier lay dying. The SS soldier is a twenty-one-year-old German from Stuttgart named Karl Seidl. Karl has asked the nurse to "bring him a Jew." Karl has been mortally wounded in battle and now wants to make his dying confession—and he wants to make it to a Jew. The SS man is wrapped in bandages covering his entire face, with only holes for his mouth, nose, and ears. For the next several hours, Simon sits alone in silence with Karl as the dying SS soldier tells his story. Karl was an only child from a Christian home. His parents had raised him in the church and had not been supporters of the Nazi party and Hitler's rise to power. But at fifteen, against his parents' wishes, Karl joined the Hitler Youth. At eighteen Karl joined the infamous SS troops.

Now as Karl is dying, he wants to confess the atrocities he has witnessed and in which he, as a Nazi SS soldier, has participated. Most horrifying is his account of being part of a group of SS soldiers sent to round up Jews in the city of Dnepropetrovsk. Three hundred Jews—men, women, children, and infants—were gathered and driven with whips into a small three-story house. The house was set on fire, and Karl recounted what happened to his confessor in these words:

> "We heard screams and saw the flames eat their way from floor to floor.... We had our rifles ready to shoot down anyone who tried to escape from that blazing hell.... The screams from that house were horrible.... Behind the windows of the second floor, I saw a man with a small child in his arms. His clothes were alight. By his side stood a woman, doubtless the mother of the child. With his free hand the man covered the child's eyes... then he jumped into the street. Seconds later the mother followed. Then from the other windows fell burning bodies... We shot... Oh God!"[2]

Karl is most haunted by the boy he shot, a boy with "dark eyes" who Karl guessed was about six years old. Karl's description of this boy reminds Simon Wiesenthal of a boy he knew in the Lemberg Ghetto.

During the several hours that Simon the Jew sat with Karl the Nazi, Simon never spoke. At Karl's request, Simon held the dying man's hand. Simon brushed away the flies and gave Karl a drink of water, but he never spoke. During the long ordeal, Simon never doubted Karl's sincerity or that he was truly sorry for his crimes. Simon said that the way Karl spoke was proof enough of his repentance. At last Karl said:

> "I am left here with my guilt. In the last hours of my life you are here with me. I do not know who you are,

5

> I only know that you are a Jew and that is enough....I
> know that what I have told you is terrible. In the long
> nights while I have been waiting for death, time and
> time again I have longed to talk about it to a Jew and
> beg forgiveness from him. Only I didn't know if there
> were any Jews left....I know that what I am asking is
> almost too much for you, but without your answer I
> cannot die in peace."[3]

With that, Simon Wiesenthal made up his mind and left
the room in silence. During all the hours that Simon Wiesenthal had sat with Karl, Simon never uttered a word. That night
Karl Seidl died. Karl left his possessions to Simon, but Simon
refused them. Against all odds, Simon Wiesenthal survived
the Holocaust. Eighty-nine members of his family did not.
But Simon Wiesenthal could not forget Karl Seidl. After the
war Simon visited Karl's mother to check out Karl's story. It
was just as Karl had said. Karl's mother assured Simon that
her son was "a good boy" and could never have done anything
bad. Again, this time out of kindness, Simon remained silent.
Simon believed that in his boyhood, Karl might indeed have
been "a good boy." But Simon also concluded that a graceless
period of his life had turned him into a murderer.

Simon Wiesenthal concludes his riveting and haunting story
with an equally riveting and haunting question addressed to
the reader.

> Ought I to have forgiven him?...Was my silence at
> the bedside of the dying Nazi right or wrong? This is
> a profound moral question that challenges the con-
> science of the reader of this episode, just as much as
> it once challenged my heart and mind....The crux of
> the matter is, of course, the question of forgiveness.
> Forgetting is something that time alone takes care of,

but forgiveness is an act of volition, and only the suf-
ferer is qualified to make the decision. You, who have
just read this sad and tragic episode in my life, can
mentally change places with me and ask yourself the
crucial question, "What would I have done?"[4]

Is Forgiveness Always Possible?

And thus we are faced with a dramatic challenge to the possibilities of forgiveness. Is forgiveness always possible? Are there
some situations in which forgiveness is impossible? Is this one
of them? Can a dying, apparently repentant Nazi find forgiveness for his sins? Can a dying SS soldier who participated in
Holocaust atrocities find forgiveness from God? And perhaps
more challengingly, can he find forgiveness from his fellow
humans? Would it even be permissible to offer forgiveness in
this case, or would it be a betrayal of justice? These are the
kind of questions that are raised by Simon Wiesenthal's *The
Sunflower*.

The second part of *The Sunflower* is a symposium of fifty-
three prominent thinkers—Jews, Christians, atheists, philosophers, professors, rabbis, ministers, and others—who respond
to Wiesenthal's question. The respondents understood the real
question as this: Is there a way that a person in Simon Wiesenthal's position could offer forgiveness of some kind to the
dying Nazi? By my count, twenty-eight of the respondents said
no, offering forgiveness in this situation is not possible. Sixteen
of the respondents said yes, there was some way in which forgiveness could have been offered. Nine of the respondents were
unclear on their positions. Interestingly, the sixteen who were
in favor of some form of forgiveness were all Christians or
Buddhists (thirteen Christians and three Buddhists). Among
Jews, Muslims, and atheists who responded there appeared to
be unanimity in agreeing that an offer of forgiveness in this
situation was impossible.

Conversely, most of the Christian respondents said there was a way in which forgiveness could be offered. Significantly, no Christian stated that forgiveness in this situation would be categorically impossible. It can't help but be noted that a Christian worldview apparently radically influences how a person approaches the possibilities of forgiveness. And it should be stressed that forgiveness here does not mean pardon in a legal sense. Had Karl Seidl lived, he still would have been subject to the demands of legal justice despite any offer of personal forgiveness. Forgiveness here should be understood not as legal pardon but an invitation back into the human community. We will explore the relationship of forgiveness and justice later.

After surviving the Holocaust and publishing *The Sunflower* in 1969, Simon Wiesenthal went on to live a noble and humanitarian life. He died in 2005 at the age of ninety-six. In *The Sunflower*, Mr. Wiesenthal does a masterful job telling his story, and his question about the possibilities of forgiveness is important for all human beings, but supremely so for Christians, because forgiveness is at the heart of the Christian faith.

On the cover of my copy of *The Sunflower* is this question: "You are a prisoner in a concentration camp. A dying Nazi soldier asks you for forgiveness. What should you do?" I felt it was important that I try to compose an answer. So even though Simon Wiesenthal never personally asked me his question, here is my unsolicited reply:

Dear Mr. Wiesenthal,

First of all let me say I will not presume to sit in judgment of your actions. You showed kindness to a dying Nazi soldier as you held his hand, brushed away the flies, and gave him water to drink. You showed great kindness to his mother in not destroying the memory of her son. And I agree with Lutheran theologian Martin Marty who says, "Non-Jews and perhaps especially Christians should not give advice about the Holocaust experience to its heirs for the next two thousand years. And then we shall have nothing to say. Cheap instant advice from a Christian would trivialize the lives and deaths of millions." Nevertheless, since you ask the question, let me try to reply. I cannot say what I would have done, only what I could hope I would have done. As a Christian I would hope that I would reply in something of this manner to my dying enemy:

"I cannot offer you forgiveness on behalf of those who have suffered monstrous crimes at your hands and the hands of those with whom you willingly aligned yourself; I have no right to speak on their behalf. But what I can tell you is that forgiveness is possible. There is a way for you to be reconciled with God, whose image you have defiled, and there is a way for you to be restored to the human race, from which you have fallen. There is a way because the One who never committed a crime cried from the cross saying, 'Father, forgive them, for they know not what they do.' Because I believe in the death, burial, and resurrection of Jesus Christ, I believe that your sin does not have to be a dead end, that there is a way forward into reconciliation.

"The forgiveness of which I speak is not a cheap forgiveness. It is not cheap because it was not cheap for Jesus Christ to suffer the violence of the cross and offer no retaliation but love and forgiveness. It is not a cheap forgiveness because it requires of you deep repentance, including a commitment to restorative justice for those you have wronged. There is no cheap forgiveness for your sins, but there is a costly forgiveness. If you in truth turn from your sins in sorrow and look to Christ in faith, there is forgiveness—a costly forgiveness that can reconcile you to God and restore you to the human race. I cannot forgive you on behalf of others, but on my own behalf and in the name of Jesus Christ, I tell you, your sins are forgiven you. Welcome to the forgiving community of forgiven sinners. May the peace of Jesus Christ be with you."

This is what I hope I would have said. But for all I know, I might have treated a dying enemy with far less kindness than you did.

IN DEEP ADMIRATION OF YOUR DIGNITY,
BRIAN ZAHND

As I read the responses from the twenty-eight or so who argued against the possibility of offering forgiveness to the dying Nazi, I found many of their arguments very compelling. Nevertheless, I'm convinced that if forgiveness is impossible for a repentant war criminal simply because his sins are too terrible, then the Christian gospel is a fairy tale, and we might as well abandon the charade. But as the Apostles' Creed says, "I believe in the forgiveness of sins." Christianity is a faith of forgiveness.

- The Christian life is a prayer of forgiveness: "Forgive us as we forgive them."
- The Christian life is a suffering cry of forgiveness: "Father, forgive them."
- The Christian life is a commission to forgive: "If you forgive anyone, they are forgiven."

So even in the face of Simon Wiesenthal's challenging question and the sympathy I may feel for those who argue that forgiveness could not be offered by a Jew to a dying Nazi, I am fully convinced that to deny the possibility of forgiveness is to deny the very heart of the Christian gospel. The oft-quoted words of Jesus, "with God all things are possible,"* not only include forgiveness but also especially pertain to forgiveness. And the call of Christ to take up our cross and follow him is very specifically a call to love our enemies and end the cycle of revenge by responding with forgiveness.

> *I'm convinced that if forgiveness is impossible for a repentant war criminal simply because his sins are too terrible, then the Christian gospel is a fairy tale, and we might as well abandon the charade.*

Of course there is a cheap forgiveness that is worthless and an affront to justice. Essentially, the Buddhist position is that evil is a nonexistent illusion, so there is really nothing to forgive. This is nothing like the Christian position. Christian forgiveness is not a cheap denial of the reality of evil or the trite sloganeering of "forgive and forget." That may suffice for minor personal affronts, but it is hollow and even insulting when applied to crimes like murder, rape, and genocide. No, Christian forgiveness is not cheap. Rather it is costly because it flows from the cross—the place where injustice and forgiveness meet in a violent collision. Christian forgiveness does not call us to forget. Christian forgiveness allows us to remember but calls us to end the cycle of revenge.

---

* Matthew 19:26

Lessons From the Master

I have found it very interesting to ask non-Christians what Jesus taught. Nearly without exception they will mention that Jesus taught us to love our enemies. Among nonbelievers, Jesus seems to be famous for teaching that his disciples should love their enemies. Yet when I ask Christians what Jesus taught, they very rarely bring up this commandment. But I think the intuition of the non-Christian is correct—Jesus's emphasis on loving enemies is central to Jesus's teaching and is especially prominent in the Sermon on the Mount. The command to love your enemy is memorable because it is radical. But the command to love your enemy is a command that we who are followers of Christ tend to *forget* because it is so very hard to do.

Yet Sermon on the Mount Christianity is the very kind of Christianity that can change the world. The Christlike love that absorbs the blow and responds with forgiveness is the only real hope this world has for real change. To respond to hate with hate enshrines the status quo and only guarantees that hate will win—it's what keeps the world as it is. We tend to think that our hatred of our enemies is justified because we can point to their obvious crimes, and, as the logic goes, if we were in charge instead of our enemies, things would be different. But history tells a different story. Hatred, no matter how justifiable, simply fuels the endless cycle of revenge. Nothing really changes except that lines on a map get redrawn. Meet the new boss; same as the old boss. Christianity has more to offer the world than recycled revenge.

September 11, 2001, is testament to the power of hate. On that day, nineteen men filled with hate and armed with box cutters changed the world. Think about that.

- Nineteen men
- Box cutters

- Hate
- Changed the world

It seems almost incredible, but it seems to be true.

Yet as followers of Jesus Christ, we are called to believe in the radical proposition that love is more powerful than hate. We are called to believe that although hatred may be very powerful, it's love that never fails, and that love is the greatest thing of all. If we hate our enemies because they first hated us, and return hate for hate because that's what hate does, we will continue to live in the ugly world of hate and its endless cycle of revenge. But when love enters the world of hate and is willing to love even its enemies, a new and real kind of change comes to the world—a change where hate does not have the last word. Yes, nineteen men full of hate and armed with box cutters changed the world. Or did they? Did the world change, or was that day simply the addition of the latest chapter in the long legacy of hate? Maybe the world didn't change at all; maybe it's just the same old thing that's been happening since Cain killed Abel.

Jesus Christ taught us to love our enemies and to pray for those who abuse us. And he modeled it to the extreme. He carried his cross to Calvary and there forgave his enemies. As Christians, we believe that Calvary is the time and place that the world began to change. Did nineteen men full of hate and armed with box cutters change the world? What about twelve men full of love and armed with forgiveness? Yes, in the Upper Room on the evening of the Resurrection, Jesus breathed upon his disciples and said, "Receive the Holy Spirit. If you forgive the sins of any, they are forgiven."* Loving and forgiving our enemies, this is how we are to change the world!

During the Armenian Genocide of 1915–1917, one and a

---

* John 20:22–23

half million Armenians were murdered by Ottoman Turks, and millions more were raped, brutalized, and forcibly deported. From the Armenian Genocide comes a famous story of a Turkish army officer who led a raid upon the home of an Armenian family. The parents were killed, and their daughters raped. The girls were then given to the soldiers. The officer kept the oldest daughter for himself. Eventually this girl was able to escape and later trained to become a nurse. In an ironic twist of fate, she found herself working in a ward for wounded Turkish army officers. One night by the dim glow of a lantern, she saw among her patients the face of the man who had murdered her parents and so horribly abused her sisters and herself. Without exceptional nursing he would die. And that is what the Armenian nurse gave—exceptional care. As the officer began to recover, a doctor pointed to the nurse and told the officer, "If it weren't for this woman, you would be dead."

The officer looked at the nurse and asked, "Have we met?"

"Yes," she replied.

After a long silence the officer asked, "Why didn't you kill me?"

The Armenian Christian replied, "I am a follower of him who said, 'Love your enemies.'"[5]

She simply said, "I am a follower of him who said, 'Love your enemies.'" For this Christian, no further explanation was necessary. For her, forgiveness was not an option; it was a requirement. Do we carry the same conviction? Do we see the practice of forgiveness as synonymous with being a Christian? When grappling with the question of forgiveness, we eventually have to grapple with the question of what it means to be a follower of Jesus. It's all too easy to reduce being a Christian to a conferred status—the result of having "accepted Jesus as your personal Savior." But that kind of minimalist approach is a gross distortion of what the earliest followers of Jesus understood being a Christian to mean. The original Christians didn't merely (or even primarily) see themselves as those who had received a "get out of hell free" card from Jesus but as followers, students, learners, and disciples of the one whom they called Master and Teacher. Jesus was the master, and they were the disciples.

Be a Disciple of Jesus

What does it mean to be a disciple? If someone were a disciple of the sitar master Ravi Shankar, it would be assumed that they hoped to learn to play the sitar with great skill. If someone were a disciple of a kung fu master, it would be assumed that they hope to eventually master the art of kung fu. So, if we call ourselves disciples of Jesus, what is it we are trying to learn? What is it that Jesus offers to teach us when we heed the call to follow him? What is Jesus the master of, which we seek to learn? The answer is "Life." Jesus is the master of living well, living rightly, living truly. Jesus is the master of living a human life as God intended. And at the center of Jesus's teaching on how we should live is the recurring theme of love and forgiveness.

For those who are serious about being a disciple of Jesus, serious about learning to live the way he taught, the Sermon on the Mount is of supreme importance. This is where Jesus sets forth his radical vision of how we should live. And make no mistake about it; it is radical—so radical that for much of Christian history, the church has occupied theologians in finding ways to get around it. Some theologians have suggested that Jesus never actually expected us to live the Sermon on the Mount; rather it was a disingenuous teaching to "drive us to grace." As the argument goes, in attempting to live the Sermon on the Mount we would find it simply can't be done, and then we would look to grace as an alternative to obeying Christ. Not grace to live the Sermon on the Mount, but grace *not* to live it.

15

This interpretation is pretty far-fetched, to say the least, but surprisingly common. Other theologians have argued that the Sermon on the Mount should be viewed as attitudes of the heart, but not as commandments to be actually obeyed. So that as long as you have the attitude of love in your heart, you don't have to actually go the second mile or actually turn the other cheek. I suppose this means that when you are treated unkindly you can retaliate like everyone else, but you are to do so with a "kindly attitude" in your heart. Of course this turns Christianity into nothing more than a nice religion of private piety—something that has been regularly done throughout the centuries. But we should keep in mind that Jesus was not crucified for teaching people to have a cheerful attitude. Jesus was crucified for teaching there was another way to live than adhering to the pharisaical religion of Israel or the brutal empire of Rome. It should be obvious from an honest reading of the Gospels that Jesus expected his disciples to master the lessons he taught and actually live a life centered on love and forgiveness. And Jesus expects his modern-day followers to do the same—to become disciples of love who master the art of forgiveness. Jesus was under no illusion that this is an easy life. In his sermon he called it a narrow and difficult road, but he also called it the road that leads to life.

The most common and vigorous protest against any serious attempt to live the Sermon on the Mount is that it's not "practical."

Not practical?

Practical is a very utilitarian (and at times ugly) word. In this case, it is code for complicity with the status quo and accepting the world *as is* as the only legitimate vision for humanity. Before we can even try to live the Sermon on the Mount, we must first experience the liberation of our imagination. If we only listen to the "practical" men who run the world as it is, we will end up settling for the anemic interpretation that the Sermon on the Mount is about private attitudes of the heart and not about Jesus's radical vision of love and forgiveness.

> *It should be obvious from an honest reading of the Gospels that Jesus expected his disciples to master the lessons he taught and actually live a life centered on love and forgiveness.*

We must keep in mind that we are told the Sermon on the Mount is not practical by those who have a deep commitment to (and perhaps a vested interest in) perpetuating the status quo. These practical men seek to control not only the way the world is run but even our imaginations. They tell us, "This is just the way the real world works," and thus they seek to confine Jesus to a "heavenly" kingdom while they get on with the practical business of running the "real" world. But the Holy Spirit is a liberator of imagination, and we must reject the arrogant pretense of the principalities and powers along with their bloody pragmatism. The church with a Christ-inspired vision and a Holy Spirit–liberated imagination is to be that realm where the followers of Jesus prove the practical men wrong by actually living the Sermon on the Mount. To live the Sermon on the Mount, we first have to rebel against the powers that be. We have to believe that there is another way of being human. We have to believe that Jesus taught and modeled that way.

The twentieth century was one of the bloodiest and most hate-filled centuries in human history. It was a century defined by war, especially the two great World Wars—The War to End All Wars…and the one that came after that. As the children who were born at the close of World War II came of age, they began to imagine an alternative to the hate and war that had defined their parents' generation, and so they sang and spoke of "love and peace." The problem was that no one could actually live it. As Larry Norman wryly observed, "Beatles said all you need is love, and then they broke up."[6] The "love and peace" generation of the sixties wasn't wrong in trying to imagine something better than a world filled with hate and war—it was wrong in not finding a better messiah than the Beatles. Jesus didn't just talk about love and peace; *he lived it to the extreme.* When Jesus prayed for his enemies to be forgiven as they drove the nails into his hands, he was living his own sermon and validating his right to preach it. After that, no one could dare claim that Jesus's teaching was not "practical." Jesus had lived it, died for it, and been vindicated by God in resurrection. His call is as vibrant and exciting today as it was two thousand years ago when he first issued it to Galilean fishermen: "Follow me." It's an invitation to follow Jesus in his radical way of enemy-love and costly forgiveness.

> *The church with a Christ-inspired vision*
> *and a Holy Spirit-liberated imagination*
> *is to be that realm where the followers of*
> *Jesus prove the practical men wrong by*
> *actually living the Sermon on the Mount.*

If the only way of responding to the evil of injustice is retaliation and revenge, we conspire with the powers of darkness to keep the world an ugly place. This is why Jesus (upon his own authority!) dared to countermand the Torah and alter the law of "an eye for an eye and a tooth for a tooth" with his radical command not to resist the one who is evil and to turn the other cheek. A world in which tit-for-tat retaliation is the rule remains an ugly place where too many people are missing an eye and a tooth. Or, as Mahatma Gandhi observed, "An eye for an eye makes the whole world blind." Jesus's vision is to end the ugliness of revenge and make the world beautiful through grace.

Grace—the Christian Alternative to Retaliation

Grace is the distinctly Christian alternative to the tired system of retaliation that perpetuates pain and leaves the whole world blind. Grace is God's idea of how the world can be made new. Grace is why Jesus could call the poor and persecuted...the mournful and meek...blessed. Jesus's entire life and message were the embodiment of the grace that triumphs over the cold pragmatism of a world where the strong dominate the weak. Jesus's message of love and forgiveness is not rooted in a naive optimism but in the grace that takes the blame, covers the shame, and removes the stain and the endless cycle of revenge.

Grace is the antidote for the Eastern concept of karma. Karma is the ancient idea that what goes around comes around, and there is no escape from it, that retribution always has the final word. But grace travels outside the rules of karma and gives a different final word. Of course, the very basis of the Christian gospel is that, because of what Christ accomplished on the cross, there is a way for sinners to be saved from the destructive consequences (karma) of their sins. But Christians are not just recipients of forgiving grace; we are also called to be those who extend the grace of forgiveness to others. Christians are to be carriers of grace in a world cursed with karma and endless cycles of revenge.

Grace is the great treasure of the kingdom of God, or as Jesus described it in his parable, a pearl of great price. That pearl is the gospel of the kingdom of heaven. It's the pearl of the gospel of grace that makes beauty out of ugly things. That's what grace does. Karma doesn't have the final word, and the ugliness of vengeance is not the final mark left upon humanity. What could be more ugly than the murder and rape of a helpless Armenian family at the hands of Turkish soldiers? Yet from that ugly episode emerges a beautiful story of grace and forgiveness.

> *Jesus's message of love and forgiveness is not rooted in a naïve optimism but in the grace that takes the blame, covers the shame, and removes the stain and the endless cycle of revenge.*

So, ultimately, for the committed Christ follower, the question of forgiveness is not a question of whether forgiveness is possible, but a question of how we can find the grace to offer forgiveness. We may discover that we offer forgiveness to transgressors and offenders the same way that Jesus did—amidst great suffering. In our feelings-oriented culture, it's easy to equate forgiveness with having certain feelings. Forgiveness is not a feeling. Forgiveness is a choice to end the cycle of revenge and leave justice in the hands of God. Very often we forgive our enemies by entering into the sufferings of Christ who forgave from the cross. As Dietrich Bonhoeffer says in *The Cost of Discipleship*, "The call to follow Christ always means a call to share the work of forgiving men their sins. Forgiveness is the Christlike suffering which it is the Christian's duty to bear."[7] Dietrich Bonhoeffer was no starry-eyed idealist who didn't know about the reality of evil. He wrote these words during the rise of Nazism in Germany and would eventually die at the hands of the Nazis. Bonhoeffer's theology of forgiveness was forged in the crucible of real and costly suffering, but for Bonhoeffer, the cost of discipleship settled the question of forgiveness.

2

The POSSIBILITY of FORGIVENESS

I N THE PREVIOUS chapter we saw that forgiveness raises many questions, and that in certain situations forgiveness can be very, very difficult. But that doesn't mean forgiveness, in general, is questioned—rather it is the extent of forgiveness that is questioned. The issue isn't whether forgiveness is a good thing—most people believe it is. The issue is how far we should go in forgiving. I suppose no one lives without occasionally offering some measure of forgiveness to those around him. To live without ever extending forgiveness, for at least minor infringements, would seem to make it nearly impossible to get on in life with any kind of normalcy. The burden of holding on to every perceived slight or imagined infraction would make life unbearable. Even the most coldhearted and embittered soul may forgive someone for stepping on his or her toes. To maintain even the most cursory level of social interaction, there must be a willingness to overlook the occasional trifling affront. The real question is: To what extent are we expected to forgive? How far shall we go in forgiving? How much can be forgiven? How often can we forgive? What are the possibilities of forgiveness?

This seemed to be the question in Peter's mind when he asked Jesus, "How often will my brother sin against me, and I forgive him?"* And before Jesus has an opportunity to answer, Peter puts forth his own idea regarding the extent of forgiveness—"As many as seven times?" I have little doubt that Peter was feeling quite generous and was rather pleased by what he perceived as a magnanimous offer of forgiveness—forgiveness times seven! Seven is a divine number, so surely forgiving seven times must be considered a divine act and would fill up the possibility of forgiveness. Surely one would not be expected to go beyond forgiving an offender seven times. But we should know by now that our presumption about what Jesus will say and our assumption that he will endorse our opinion are almost always misplaced. Jesus is the Christ of perpetual surprise, and those who walk with Jesus soon discover this. Peter certainly did. Can you imagine Peter's astonishment when Jesus said, "I do not say to you seven times, but seventy times seven."† *Seventy times seven!* Peter didn't see that coming.

Interestingly, there is some uncertainty among New Testament translators as to whether Jesus meant seventy-seven or seventy sevens (70 x 7). Did Jesus mean seventy *plus* seven or seventy *times* seven? Is Jesus talking about adding to forgiveness or multiplying forgiveness? The Greek text is ambiguous. The New International Version and the New Revised Standard Version translate it as seventy-seven, while most other translations understand it as seventy times seven. I am of the opinion that Jesus meant seventy *times* seven, not because of something in the Greek text, but because of something in the Old Testament Book of Daniel. Jesus, of course, was very familiar with

---

* Matthew 18:21
† Matthew 18:22

the Book of Daniel. In fact, it seems to have been a very important book to Jesus. He often spoke of the kingdom of God and used for himself the title of the Son of Man—both are themes that originated in this book. It was the prophecies of Daniel that provided Jesus with an eschatological framework for his ministry and an apocalyptic understanding of his times. In the mysterious ninth chapter of Daniel, the angel Gabriel speaks of seventy weeks decreed for Israel, or literally seventy sevens.

> Seventy "sevens" are decreed for your people and your holy city to finish transgression, to put an end to sin, to atone for wickedness, to bring in everlasting righteousness, to seal up vision and prophecy and to anoint the most holy.
> —DANIEL 9:24, NIV

When the angel Gabriel speaks to Daniel about something decreed for Israel that will finish transgression, put an end to sin, atone for wickedness, and bring in everlasting righteousness, he speaks of seventy *times* seven. Whatever eschatological meaning we may want to apply to the seventy weeks (sevens), it should be clear that seventy times seven is related to atonement, forgiveness, and the establishment of everlasting righteousness. Seventy times seven becomes an equation connected with how humanity moves beyond transgression and retribution into the new world of forgiveness and restoration. As Jesus so often alluded to Daniel's prophecies when referring to himself, I think there is little doubt that he was aware of the significance of seventy times seven. Jesus's response to Peter was not arbitrary. Jesus understood that if atonement is to prevail over transgression, then, according to Daniel's prophecy, seventy times seven must be our vision for the possibilities of forgiveness. What I am suggesting is that there is more than a coincidental link between Daniel's seventy times seven and Jesus's seventy times seven—the two 490s in the Bible. Very interestingly, there is another variation on this theme in the Bible—Lamech's vengeful seventy-sevenfold.

> I have killed a man for wounding me,
>> a young man for striking me.
> If Cain's revenge is sevenfold,
>> then Lamech's is seventy-sevenfold.
>> —GENESIS 4:23–24

Lamech's lust for revenge to be increased from sevenfold to seventy-sevenfold is humanity headed in the wrong direction. It leads to a world that is corrupt, filled with violence, and doomed to destruction—a destruction that came in the next generation with the flood of Noah's day. The lesson should be clear—the lust for revenge and the corresponding exponential increase of retaliation leads to a world filled with corruption and violence and doomed to destruction. The only way to put an end to sin and restore the world is if forgiveness can be multiplied exponentially. Seventy times seven.

Even if we don't want to think about forgiveness on a global or cosmic scale, preferring to keep our consideration regarding the possibilities of forgiveness to a personal level, there's no getting around the fact that Jesus challenges our limited ideas regarding the extent of forgiveness. Not seven times. Seventy times seven!

When Jesus says to Peter (and to us) not seven times, but seventy times seven, what is he saying? Isn't he saying that we must always find a way to forgive? Isn't he suggesting that the possibilities of forgiveness are endless? That to be sinned against is to be called to forgive? Yes, I believe this is precisely what Jesus is calling us to. Make no mistake about it; this call to forgiveness is extreme. It's a call that transcends the bounds of what casually can be considered as reasonable. To follow Jesus as a disciple is to become a practitioner of radical forgiveness.

Conventional forgiveness, easy forgiveness, reasonable forgiveness is what most rationally minded people are willing to engage in. Christ's followers are called to radical forgiveness, unreasonable forgiveness, reckless forgiveness, endless forgiveness, seemingly impossible forgiveness. The expectations regarding forgiveness that Jesus places upon his disciples are among the most demanding aspects of Christian discipleship, but these demands must not be ignored.

When Peter suggests sevenfold forgiveness, he is being generous and going well beyond what most are willing to do. Forgive the same person for the same offense seven times? Who would dare ask any more of us? Well, Jesus does. Jesus dares to ask more of us. Jesus calls his disciples to the radical extreme of seventy times seven. He calls us to push the boundaries of forgiveness far beyond all that seems reasonable. This point needs to be very clear in your thinking—Jesus was *not* repeating the admonitions of conventional wisdom. Jesus was *not* calling for a kind of forgiveness that simply belongs to human decency. Jesus was *not* endorsing a concept of forgiveness that was already present and practiced among religious people. Jesus was saying something new. Something extreme. Something radical.

Jesus Challenges the Law

Living twenty centuries after the Sermon on the Mount, it is all too easy to miss how shocking this sermon actually is. The Beatitudes are not platitudes of conventional wisdom—they are the deeply counterintuitive wisdom of God challenging our most basic assumptions. The whole Sermon on the Mount was (and is!) a bold challenge to the accepted assumptions of the day. Consider Jesus's challenge of the accepted paradigm of retaliation.

> You have heard that it was said, "An eye for an eye and
> a tooth for a tooth." But I say to you, Do not resist the
> one who is evil. But if anyone slaps you on the right
> cheek, turn to him the other also.
>
> —MATTHEW 5:38–39

When Jesus says repeatedly in the Sermon on the Mount,
"You have heard it said...but I say to you," he was daring to
challenge the Torah (the Jewish Scriptures). It would be tan-
tamount to a preacher today saying, "You have heard it said
in the Bible, but I say to you..." This is why Jacob Neusner,
in his book *A Rabbi Talks With Jesus*, says, "Only God can
demand of me what Jesus asks."[1] Exactly. In the Sermon on
the Mount, Jesus is making an implicit claim to speak with
the same authority as the One who gave the Law at Mount
Sinai. Jesus was saying that the Law given at Mount Sinai was
being countermanded by the sermon given at the Mount of
Beatitudes. This is why the crowd at the end of the sermon was
so shocked—Jesus did not base his sermon on the authority
of the Torah but on his *own* authority!

Upon his own authority, Jesus challenges and alters the Law
of Moses. Moses called for a reciprocal response to injustice
and injury—"life for life, eye for eye, tooth for tooth, hand for
hand, foot for foot, burn for burn, wound for wound, stripe
for stripe."* But Jesus calls for the counterintuitive response of
turning the other cheek. Instead of a reciprocal response, Jesus
calls for radical forgiveness. Turning the other cheek, though
perhaps heard as a cliché today, is still a very difficult demand
that forces us to push the boundaries on the possibilities of
forgiveness. But the Christ follower does not have the option
to choose Moses's reciprocal response over Jesus's radical

---

* Exodus 21:23–25

forgiveness. Jesus calls his disciples to a different way, a better way, a higher way, and ultimately, a necessary way.

> *Even if we don't want to think about forgiveness on a global or cosmic scale, preferring to keep the possibilities of forgiveness to a personal level, there's no getting around the fact that Jesus challenges our limited ideas regarding the extent of forgiveness.*

Yet when Jesus calls us to extend forgiveness in a radical way, we are not expected to do so through gritted teeth, but out of our own experience of being forgiven. Jesus and the apostles seem to believe that being a recipient of the infinite love of God should create within the forgiven sinner a wellspring of infinite capacity to forgive. We forgive out of our experience of being forgiven. We love infinitely out of the reality of being infinitely loved. We love with the love of God and forgive with the forgiveness we have received. We turn the other cheek because Jesus prayed from the cross, "Father, forgive them." And the forgiven *them* turns out to be us. Jesus only calls us to give what we have received—unbounded forgiveness.

So Jesus is deliberately and radically expanding the possibilities of forgiveness. What Israel was expected to do with forgiveness under Moses is daringly altered by Jesus. But this call to radical forgiveness is an explicitly Christian call. We do not heed this call because it necessarily makes sense or seems reasonable, but because it is *Jesus* who calls us to it! We might dismiss the Sermon on the Mount as dangerously naïve, except that it is our Lord who gave the sermon.

As Christians we work backward from the Resurrection.

Because we believe that Jesus has been raised from the dead and vindicated by God as Lord of all, we dare not dismiss the Sermon on the Mount as pious but unrealistic platitudes. Instead we must find a way to love our enemies, turn the other cheek, and forgive seventy times seven. It is a uniquely Christian call. And it is why even though Simon Wiesenthal's challenging question about the possibility of forgiveness is to be respected, for the Christian there is ultimately only one answer—we must find a way to forgive.

> *Even though Simon Wiesenthal's challenging question about the possibility of forgiveness is to be respected, for the Christian there is ultimately only one answer—we must find a way to forgive.*

Find a Way to Forgive

Corrie ten Boom was a Dutch Christian whose family was involved in hiding and rescuing Dutch Jews during the Holocaust and the German occupation of Holland. Eventually the Nazi SS discovered their activities, and they were arrested. Corrie ten Boom's father died in prison shortly after the arrest. Corrie and her sister, Betsie, were sent to the notorious concentration camp in Ravensbrück, where they suffered from near starvation and the barbarous cruelty of the guards. Corrie's beloved sister, Betsie, died in Ravensbrück.

Following the war, Corrie returned to Holland to set up rehabilitation centers and eventually gained international recognition for her books and charitable work. In 1947 she was speaking at a church in Munich, Germany, when she met one of Ravensbrück's cruelest guards, setting the stage for a supreme test of the possibilities of forgiveness. In her book *Tramp for the Lord*, Corrie ten Boom tells the story of their encounter.

◆～◆

It was in a church in Munich that I saw him—a balding, heavyset man in a gray overcoat, a brown felt hat clutched between his hands. People were filing out of the basement room where I had just spoken, moving along the rows of wooden chairs to the door at the rear. It was 1947, and I had come from Holland to defeated Germany with the message that God forgives.

It was the truth they needed most to hear in that bitter, bombed-out land, and I gave them my favorite mental picture. Maybe because the sea is never far from a Hollander's mind, I like to think that that's where forgiven sins were thrown. "When we confess our sins," I said, "God casts them into the deepest ocean, gone forever. And even though I cannot find a Scripture for it, I believe God then places a sign out there that says, 'NO FISHING ALLOWED.'"

The solemn faces stared back at me, not quite daring to believe. There were never questions after a talk in Germany in 1947. People stood up in silence, in silence collected their wraps, in silence left the room.

And that's when I saw him, working his way forward against the others. One moment I saw the overcoat and the brown hat; the next, a blue uniform and a visored cap with its skull and crossbones. It came back with a rush: the huge room with its harsh overhead lights; the pathetic pile of dresses and shoes in the center of the floor; the shame of walking naked past this man. I could see my sister's frail form ahead of me, ribs sharp beneath the parchment skin. *Betsie, how thin you were!*

The place was Ravensbrück and the man who was making his way forward had been a guard—one of the most cruel guards.

Now he was in front of me, hand thrust out: "A fine message, Fraulein! How good it is to know that, as you say, all our sins are at the bottom of the sea!"

And I, who had spoken so glibly of forgiveness, fumbled in my pocketbook rather than take that hand. He would not remember me, of course—how could he remember one prisoner among those thousands of women?

But I remembered him and the leather crop swinging from his belt. I was face-to-face with one of my captors, and my blood seemed to freeze.

"You mentioned Ravensbrück in your talk," he was saying. "I was a guard there." No, he did not remember me.

"But since that time," he went on, "I have become a Christian. I know that God has forgiven me for the cruel things I did there, but I would like to hear it from your lips as well. Fraulein,"—again the hand came out—"will you forgive me?"

And I stood there—I whose sins had again and again to be forgiven—and could not forgive. Betsie had died in that place—could he erase her slow terrible death simply for the asking?

It could not have been many seconds that he stood there—hand held out—but to me it seemed hours as I wrestled with the most difficult thing I had ever had to do.

For I had to do it—I knew that. The message that God forgives has a prior condition: that we forgive those who have injured us. "If you do not forgive men their trespasses," Jesus says, "neither will your Father in heaven forgive your trespasses."

I knew it not only as a commandment of God, but as a daily experience. Since the end of the war I had had a home in Holland for victims of Nazi brutality. Those who were able to forgive their former enemies were able also to return to the outside world and rebuild their lives, no matter what the physical scars. Those who nursed their bitterness remained invalids. It was as simple and as horrible as that.

And still I stood there with the coldness clutching my heart. But forgiveness is not an emotion—I knew that too. Forgiveness is an act of the will, and the will can function regardless of the temperature of the heart. "Jesus, help me!" I prayed silently. "I can lift my hand. I can do that much. You supply the feeling."

And so woodenly, mechanically, I thrust my hand into the one stretched out to me. And as I did, an incredible thing took place. The current started in my shoulder, raced down my arm, sprang into our joined hands. And then this healing warmth seemed to flood my whole being, bringing tears to my eyes.

"I forgive you, brother!" I cried. "With all my heart."

For a long moment we grasped each other's hands, the former guard and the former prisoner. I had never known God's love so intensely as I did then. But even so, I realized it was not my love. I had tried, and did not have the power. It was the power of the Holy Spirit as recorded in Romans 5:5, "...because the love of God is shed abroad in our hearts by the Holy Ghost which is given to us."[2]

In the previous chapter I attempted to answer Simon Wiesenthal's question about forgiving a Nazi SS soldier in a hypothetical way. Hypothetical, because I have never suffered in a Nazi concentration camp. But Corrie ten Boom faced the question of forgiveness in stark reality. She had suffered in a Nazi death camp. She had lost family members in the Holocaust. She had experienced firsthand the cruelty of Nazi prison guards. And she was asked to forgive. She was not asked about the *possibility* of forgiveness; she was asked to *actually* forgive a Nazi who had treated her with callous cruelty and contributed to the death of her sister. And the saintly Corrie ten Boom makes two points quite clear. First, it was not easy to offer forgiveness to a Nazi tormenter, and second, as a Christian she had no choice but to do so.

But she also makes the important point that forgiveness is not an emotion; it is an act of the will. In a mechanical act of the will to obey Jesus and offer forgiveness, Corrie ten Boom discovered that the love of God through the Holy Spirit is released, thus making forgiveness genuine and transformative. This is Christianity in its essence. This is Christianity at its finest. This is Christianity, not as the conventional wisdom of civil religion, but as the counterintuitive wisdom of the Sermon on the Mount. This is the Christianity that is not a chaplain to the status quo but a catalyst for profound and positive change. This is the Christianity that can change the world!

Agents of Reconciliation

It is by the Holy Spirit that the possibilities of forgiveness are expanded to the infinite. We are not called to infinitely forgive on our own. This would be to ask the impossible. Rather we are called to make the difficult choice to forgive as an act of obedience to Jesus Christ, and then to become a channel through which the Holy Spirit brings the love of God into a deeply broken and alienated world. Christian forgiveness that extends seventy times seven is not an act of the lone individual but an act in concert with the entire Trinity. Christian forgiveness that pushes the possibilities into the infinite involves the love of God, the resurrection of Jesus Christ, and the baptism in the Holy Spirit. In a sacred dance with the Trinity, we become agents of the reconciliation whereby God is bringing healing into a world crippled by the seemingly unforgivable.

> *Christ's followers are called to radical forgiveness, unreasonable forgiveness, reckless forgiveness, endless forgiveness, seemingly impossible forgiveness.*

Tyrese is a man in our church who was born with the deck stacked against him. His father was African American, his mother was full-blooded Native American, and at the age of one he was abandoned by his parents and subsequently raised in a Muslim home. As a black, Native American, orphaned Muslim in an all-white school in a small town in Kansas, Tyrese was in many ways the ultimate outsider. And Tyrese knows full well the hostility that can be engendered from a deep sense of alienation. Ordained as a Muslim minister when he was eighteen, Tyrese began to set up Moorish Science Temples in American prisons. Islam was a way for black prisoners to find a sense of belonging while at the same time distancing themselves from the wider culture in which they felt they had no place. But what Tyrese did not find in Islam was a sense of personal forgiveness—the assurance that God had forgiven his sins. Recognizing that the brand of Islam he was importing into prisons was more gang related than genuinely religious, Tyrese abandoned his work in prisons.

In his thirties, Tyrese began to explore Christianity,

embarking on a spiritual journey that eventually led him to faith in Jesus Christ. Today Tyrese is an ordained Christian pastor who leads our prison ministry—a remarkable ministry that has seen thousands of incarcerated men and women place their faith in Jesus Christ and find the liberation of forgiveness.

> *Not only does forgiveness open new possibilities for the future, but forgiveness also gives us a new perspective on the past. In some mysterious way that we may not be able to fully comprehend, forgiveness seems to have the capacity to redeem the past.*

I remember sitting across a restaurant table from Tyrese and telling him I wanted to talk about race, religion, and politics. Tyrese comes from a heritage deeply shaped by America's two greatest sins—the atrocity of African slavery and the systematic destruction of Native Americans. Tyrese's paternal heritage arrived in America chained as cargo on slave ships, and his maternal heritage walked the Trail of Tears in a forced relocation from Mississippi to Oklahoma. Add to that the trauma of being abandoned by his parents as a toddler, and Tyrese has far more reasons than most to be embittered. But he's not. Not in the least. In fact, Tyrese is one of the most loving and kind, joyful and generous persons I know. Tyrese always greets me with a smile, a hug, and an encouraging word.

When I asked how it was that he was not bitter—not bitter at life, his family, or his nation—Tyrese explained that there was indeed a time when he carried deep bitterness. But he had been saved from his bitterness. Having received forgiveness in Jesus Christ, he understood that he now had to extend forgiveness to others. He understood the reciprocal nature of forgiveness—that we forgive as we have been forgiven. In a word, Tyrese is not bitter because he is a Christian—a Christian in the fullest sense.

As Tyrese has lived a life of forgiveness, he has seen God reconcile him with his biological parents, give him a wonderful family, and use him to bring saving grace to thousands of people in prison. Because Tyrese embraced the possibility of forgiveness, he has seen God work all things together for good in his life. When we embrace the possibility of forgiveness, we open the door for healing possibilities we would not have otherwise. Choosing the possibility of forgiveness gives us new possibilities for our life.

Not only does forgiveness open new possibilities for the future, but forgiveness also gives us a new perspective on the past. In some mysterious way that we may not be able to fully comprehend, forgiveness seems to have the capacity to redeem the past. What would otherwise poison us now has a redemptive quality in our life. This too is part of the possibility of forgiveness. Forgiveness seems to have the capacity to alter suffering from something that is purely destructive to something that has profound redemptive qualities. Few have spoken of this mysterious truth regarding redemptive suffering more eloquently than Aleksandr Solzhenitsyn.

Redemptive Suffering

Aleksandr Solzhenitsyn was born in Soviet Russia in 1918 and would eventually be known to the world as an acclaimed dissident, a brilliant author, a Nobel laureate, and an important Christian thinker. Early in his life, Solzhenitsyn had been a devoted Communist, but in 1945 he was sentenced to eight years in a Soviet labor camp for referring to Joseph Stalin as "the whiskered one" in a private letter. Solzhenitsyn would later chronicle the horrors of the gulag in his gripping novel

One Day in the Life of Ivan Denisovich, for which he won the Nobel Prize in literature.[3]

Solzhenitsyn's eight years in prison were truly horrible, yet it was while he was in prison that Solzhenitsyn was led to faith in Christ through the witness of a Jewish believer—a man who was later beaten to death by prison guards. It was the fact that he had found forgiveness while suffering unjustly in a Soviet gulag, and in response learned the grace of forgiving, that gave Aleksandr Solzhenitsyn such a redemptive perspective on his prison years. In his mammoth work *The Gulag Archipelago*—which *TIME* magazine called the best nonfiction book of the twentieth century—Solzhenitsyn brings a redemptive perspective to his personal suffering. In part IV, *The Soul and Barbed Wire*, Solzhenitsyn writes on what he calls "The Ascent."

&·∽·&

You are ascending...

Formerly you never forgave anyone. You judged people without mercy. Now an understanding mildness has become the basis of your judgments. You have come to realize your own weakness—and you can therefore understand the weakness of others.

The stones rustle beneath our feet. We are ascending...

Your soul, which formerly was dry, now ripens from suffering.

And what would one then have to say about our so evident torturers? Why does not fate punish *them*? Why do they prosper? And the only solution to this would be that the meaning of earthly existence lies not, as we have grown used to thinking, in prospering, but...in the development of the soul. From *that* point of view our torturers have been punished most horribly of all: they are turning into swine, *they are departing downward from humanity.*

It was granted me to carry away from my prison years on my bent back, which nearly broke beneath its load, this essential experience: *how* a human being becomes evil and *how* a human being becomes good. In the intoxication of youthful successes I had felt myself to be infallible, and I was therefore cruel. In my most evil moments I was convinced that I was doing good, and I was well supplied with systematic arguments. It was only when I lay there on rotting prison straw that I sensed within myself the first stirrings of good. Gradually it was disclosed to me that the line separating good and evil passes not through states, nor between classes, nor between political parties—but right through every human heart and through all human hearts. This line shifts. Inside us, it oscillates with the years. It is impossible to expel evil from the world in its entirety, but it is possible to constrict it within each person.

And that is why I turn back to the years of my imprisonment and say, sometimes to the astonishment of those about me: *"Bless you, prison!"*

I nourished my soul there, and I say without hesitation: *"Bless you, prison, for having been in my life!"*[4]

❧

Because Aleksandr Solzhenitsyn found forgiveness and learned how to forgive while suffering in prison, he was able to speak the remarkable words, "Bless you, prison, for having been in my life." The surprising possibility of forgiveness had given Solzhenitsyn a new perspective on his suffering. He spoke of his suffering as an "Ascent." Formerly he never offered forgiveness and judged others without mercy. But having found forgiveness in the context of suffering, Solzhenitsyn spoke of his soul as "ripening" and developing an "understanding mildness" that enabled him to understand and sympathize with the weaknesses of others.

I first read these words of Aleksandr Solzhenitsyn while ministering in Siberia not far from where one of the Soviet-era gulags had been located. It profoundly affected me. I regard *The Soul and Barbed Wire* as one of the most moving and brilliant things I have ever read. It forever altered the way I viewed suffering as well as the mistaken notion that the line separating good and evil can be located between groups of people (more on that in a later chapter).

> *It is forgiveness alone that has the capacity to break the chains of injustice and give us the possibility of a new future—a future unchained from the past and free of bitterness.*

But the point I wish to stress here is that Aleksandr Solzhenitsyn emerged from prison a more forgiving person, and therefore a better person. But it is not to be assumed that prison and suffering in and of themselves tend to make people better and more forgiving. They do not. People are in fact more likely to emerge from unjust imprisonment and undeserved suffering as deeply angry and embittered. Rather, it was because he had first encountered the forgiveness of sins found in Jesus Christ that Solzhenitsyn was able to develop in his "ripened soul" a capacity for forgiveness that opened to him a world of new possibilities. Having been forgiven, he began to discover the possibilities of forgiveness.

The world of resentment and bitterness is a small, ever-shrinking world. It is a world of ever-diminishing possibilities. It is a world on a trajectory of collapse into the singularity of resentment. Unforgiveness has a devastating way of eliminating new possibilities. Everything remains chained to the past, and the suffered injustice becomes the single informing event in the life of the embittered soul. But the choice to forgive breaks the tyranny of injustice and the bitterness it seeks to create.

The Discipline of Enemy-Love

The world of forgiveness is the world of new and expanding possibilities. Very often people are afraid to forgive because they assume that if they forgive, injustice will triumph. Yet the counterintuitive wisdom of Christ reveals that the very opposite is true. It is forgiveness alone that has the capacity to break the chains of injustice and give us the possibility of a new future— a future unchained from the past and free of bitterness. And this is why Jesus calls his followers to the demanding discipline of enemy-love. Again we hear challenging words of Jesus from the Sermon on the Mount.

> You have heard that it was said, "You shall love your neighbor and hate your enemy." But I say to you, Love your enemies and pray for those who persecute you, so that you may be sons of your Father who is in heaven.
> —MATTHEW 5:43–45

Nikolai Velimirović was a Serbian Orthodox bishop who, during World War II and the German occupation of Yugoslavia, taught against the evils of Nazism to the priests under his charge. He was betrayed by one of the priests, arrested, and sent to the concentration camp at Dachau. It was in Dachau that Nikolai Velimirović learned to pray for his enemy persecutors and, most of all, for the man who had betrayed him. As a prisoner in Dachau, Velimirović composed a prayer known as "Prayer Regarding Critics and Enemies."

❖⸱～⸱❖

Bless my enemies, O Lord. Even I bless them and do not curse them. Enemies have driven me into your embrace more than friends have. Friends have bound me to earth; enemies have loosed me from earth and have demolished all my aspirations in the world.

Enemies have made me a stranger in worldly realms and an extraneous inhabitant of the world.

Just as a hunted animal finds safer shelter than an unhunted animal does, so have I, persecuted by enemies, found the safest sanctuary, having ensconced myself beneath your tabernacle, where neither friends nor enemies can slay my soul.

Bless my enemies, O Lord. Even I bless and do not curse them.

They, rather than I, have confessed my sins before the world. They have punished me, whenever I have hesitated to punish myself. They have tormented me, whenever I have tried to flee torments. They have scolded me, whenever I have flattered myself. They have spat upon me, whenever I have filled myself with arrogance. Bless my enemies, O Lord. Even I bless them and do not curse them.

Whenever I have made myself wise, they have called me foolish. Whenever I have made myself mighty, they have mocked me as though I were a fly.

Whenever I have wanted to lead people, they have shoved me into the background.

Whenever I have rushed to enrich myself, they have prevented me with an iron hand.

Whenever I thought that I would sleep peacefully, they have wakened me from sleep.

Whenever I have tried to build a home for a long and tranquil life, they have demolished it and driven me out.

Truly, enemies have cut me loose from the world and have stretched out my hands to the hem of your garment.

Bless my enemies, O Lord. Even I bless them and do not curse them.

Bless them and multiply them; multiply them and make them even more bitterly against me:

So that my fleeing will have no return; So that all my hope in men may be scattered like cobwebs; So that absolute serenity may begin to reign in my soul; So that my heart may become the grave of my two evil twins: arrogance and anger;

So that I might amass all my treasure in heaven; Ah, so that I may for once be freed from self-deception, which has entangled me in the dreadful web of illusory life.

Enemies have taught me to know what hardly anyone knows, that a person has no enemies in the world except himself. One hates his enemies only when he fails to realize that they are not enemies, but cruel friends.

It is truly difficult for me to say who has done me more good and who has done me more evil in the world: friends or enemies. Therefore bless, O Lord, both my friends and my enemies. A slave curses enemies, for he does not understand. But a son blesses them, for he understands.

For a son knows that his enemies cannot touch his life. Therefore he freely steps among them and prays to

God for them. Bless my enemies, O Lord. Even I bless
them and do not curse them.[5]

❦

I'm not sure I can pray all of that prayer. I'm not sure I
want my enemies to increase. I'm not sure I want my enemies
to be even more bitterly against me. But I fully recognize that
this remarkable prayer by a Serbian Orthodox bishop is full
of deep wisdom and overflows with the kind of Christianity
firmly rooted in the Sermon on the Mount. Nearly every line
contains some of the counterintuitive wisdom that characterized the teaching of Jesus. I recognize the scent of the Holy
Spirit in this prayer. It is a prayer that reminds me of the
endless possibilities of forgiveness. It is a prayer that reminds
me that the Sermon on the Mount transcends the comfortable confines of conventional wisdom. This prayer reminds
me that the command of Christ concerning forgiveness is not
the generous offer of seven times, but the radical and absurd
commitment to forgive seventy times seven.

3

The IMITATION OF CHRIST

O N THE NORTHEAST side of Jerusalem's Old City there is a gate leading to the Via Dolorosa known as St. Stephen's Gate. It is so named because it's believed to be near the site where the first Christian martyr, St. Stephen, was stoned to death. (His story is told in Acts 7.) I've gone in and out of that gate dozens of times, and whenever I do, I can't help but think about the stoning of Stephen and his imitation of Christ as he was dying. St. Stephen's Gate is a place characterized by anger. Anger and animosity from the seemingly endless Israeli-Palestinian conflict are often in evidence around St. Stephen's Gate—it's a place where there's always tension in the air. Just today I read of another stone-throwing "incident" at that location. It's the kind of place where it's not hard to imagine an angry mob whipped into a religious frenzy unleashing their anger in violence. This is precisely what led to Stephen's death—and gave Stephen an opportunity to imitate Christ.

Stephen was a deacon who served in the Jerusalem church in the early days following Jesus's resurrection. As a preacher, he was a bold and eloquent witness that Jesus was Israel's Messiah. When Stephen was accused of blasphemy for preaching Jesus as Messiah, he was forcibly taken outside the city walls to be executed by stoning—the punishment mandated in the Torah for blasphemers. As the stones began to fly, Stephen began to pray a remarkable prayer. Stephen's prayer is a stunning imitation of Christ, who, a few years earlier and not far from where Stephen was being executed, had prayed, "Father, forgive them, for they know not what they do."* Stephen's prayer was similar. It was not an imprecatory prayer calling down curses upon his persecutors, but a prayer of forgiveness. Stephen's last words were these: "Lord, do not hold this sin against them."† What an impeccable imitation of Christ! We find Stephen, with his dying breath, praying for the forgiveness of those who were unjustly putting him to death. Stephen, like Jesus, worked miracles, but Stephen never more fully imitated Christ than in his dying prayer of forgiveness.

Forgive or Avenge?

I want to contrast Jesus's and Stephen's dying prayers of forgiveness with the famous dying words of Matthathias. Matthathias was a Jewish priest in the second century B.C. and was the father of the Jewish hero Judah Maccabeus. At this time, the Jewish nation was oppressed by the Greek Seleucid king Antiochus Epiphanes. A revolt was sparked against the Seleucids in 167 B.C. when Matthathias killed a Hellenistic Jew who volunteered to offer a sacrifice to the Greek gods. A year later when Matthathias was put to death, he charged his sons to: "Avenge the wrong done to your people. Pay back the Gentiles in full."[1]

Matthathias' third son, Judah Maccabeus, became the

---

*   Luke 23:34

†   Acts 7:60

leader of a somewhat successful guerilla war against the Seleucid oppressors. (*Maccabeus* means "Hammer.") Many Jews thought that perhaps he was the Messiah they'd been waiting and hoping for. But it was not to be. Judah Maccabeus ended up forming a treaty with the Romans, and the Romans ended up being just as oppressive as the Greeks. One hundred sixty years later, when a baby was born in Bethlehem and laid in a manger, Judah the Hammer was the prototype for the avenging Messiah that Israel was expecting to show up at any time. The Maccabeus version of Messiah was a righter of wrongs who would issue paybacks, take up the sword, and prevail in battle against Israel's Gentile oppressors. In the first century A.D., Israel longed for the second coming of Judah the Hammer who would deliver them from their current oppressors, the Romans.

But Jesus of Nazareth did not fit the Judah Maccabeus prototype—he did not come as an avenging Messiah. He did not come to issue paybacks. He did not come to take up the sword or bring the hammer down on Israel's national enemies. Jesus didn't come to be the second coming of "The Hammer." And this is partly why Israel's religious and political elite rejected Jesus as Messiah—he did not fit the predetermined expectation of an avenging Messiah. Jesus wasn't the Hammer of God; he was the Lamb of God.

But it wasn't only the religious and political elite in the first-century society of Israel who looked and longed for an avenging Messiah—a Messiah who would bring the hammer down on Israel's national enemies. This angry, avenging attitude was also prevalent among Jesus's own disciples. When a Samaritan village rejected Jesus, the disciples James and John—whom Jesus had aptly nicknamed "Sons of Thunder"—wanted to call down fire from heaven and avenge the insult. Jesus rebuked the Sons of Thunder, telling them they didn't know what kind of spirit was motivating them. James and John had to learn that Jesus was not a messiah who would "shock and awe" his enemies with the hammer of violence. Instead he had come to love and forgive his enemies.

Jesus's revolutionary manifesto was not the stirring war speech of Matthathias but the deeply counterintuitive Sermon on the Mount. But many, quite frankly, were disappointed in this "weak" version of Messiah. Even among Jesus's own disciples the disappointment was evident. Perhaps this is why Peter denied knowing Jesus after his arrest in the Garden of Gethsemane. He was ready to fight to the death, and he drew his sword and cut off the ear of a soldier arresting Jesus. He must have been bitterly disappointed and disillusioned when Jesus told him to put away the sword and allowed himself to be taken without a fight. It was only after the Resurrection that the disciples changed their opinion and recognized that God had vindicated this *weak* Messiah and made him King of kings and Lord of lords.

Judah Maccabeus was the Hammer of God. Jesus of Nazareth was the Lamb of God. They are competing visions of Messiah. One is an avenging messiah bringing the hammer down on Israel's national enemies. The other is a Suffering Servant laying his life down as a lamb to be slaughtered. One perpetuates the cycle of revenge with his hammer. The other ends the cycle of revenge with his cross. We must choose which vision of Messiah we will embrace. Heaven issues its verdict when it declares, "Worthy is the Lamb."*

If Jesus had satisfied the lust for vengeance present in Israel's nationalistic agenda by becoming a militant Messiah like Judah Maccabeus, nothing really would have changed. No doubt Jesus *could* have led Israel to a military victory over its Roman oppressors, but that would only have perpetuated the bloody cycle of vengeance. Instead of Babylon, Persia, Greece,

---

* Revelation 5:12

or Rome being the monstrous oppressor, Israel would have had its turn at ruling the world with the sword. But what would that have changed? Nothing really—just the name of the latest ruling empire: "Meet the new boss, same as the old boss." Jesus didn't come to conquer the world with a sword; he came to save the world with a cross. Jesus didn't come to perpetuate the system of revenge; he came to end the bloody and vicious cycle of paybacks by absorbing the blow and forgiving enemies. He came to reconcile Jews and Gentiles into one new humanity, a new humanity formed at the cross.[*]

> *Jesus didn't come to conquer the world with a sword; he came to save the world with a cross.*

And this is the Messiah whom Stephen dared to imitate when, instead of calling out for vengeance as Matthathias had done, he prayed that his executioners be forgiven, as Jesus had done. Stephen didn't justify the unjust actions of those who were stoning him (he called it sin), but he asked that this sin not be charged to them. A crime was committed against Stephen, but before God, Stephen did not want to press charges. Amazing! It's the imitation of Christ.

A Living Imitation of Christ

When we choose to forgive those who intentionally and maliciously harm us instead of perpetuating the cycle of revenge, we become a living imitation of Jesus Christ. And as we do this, we help flood a world hell-bent on paybacks with a forgiveness that washes away sin. The world is all too full of the lust for vengeance. This lust is ultimately demonic in nature

---

[*] Ephesians 2:12

and is what fuels all our wars—from petty personal conflicts to deadly world wars. Christians are called to opt out of the game of getting even. The saying is that "vengeance is sweet," but vengeance is sweet only to the sick soul. To those who have tasted the grace of God in Christ, vengeance is bitter as gall. Bob Dylan talks about the perversity of calling revenge "sweet" in his underappreciated song "Dark Eyes."

> They tell me to be discreet for all intended purposes,
> They tell me revenge is sweet, and from where they
>   stand, I'm sure it is.
> But I feel nothing for their game where beauty goes
>   unrecognized,
> All I feel is heat and flame and all I see are dark
>   eyes.[2]

Revenge is not sweet. It's the heat and flame of hell and leads to the dark eyes of a lost soul. Those who would aspire to imitate Christ must feel nothing for the game of paybacks. The saying "paybacks are hell" is true in more than one sense. Paybacks are not only hell for the recipient of revenge; paybacks are also hell for the executioner of revenge. It's the lust for revenge that destroys our souls and keeps us chained in a devil's hell of exponential hatred and endless retribution. The only way out is the imitation of Christ.

For many people—Catholics and Protestants alike—Pope John Paul II was a living imitation of Christ. John Paul II imitated Christ in his humility, in his embrace of the poor and oppressed, and in his patient enduring of suffering. But he most fully imitated Christ when he forgave the man who had attempted to murder him.

On May 13, 1981, Mehmet Ali Agca, a Turkish Muslim, approached Pope John Paul II as he traveled in an open motorcade through St. Peter's Square in Rome. Standing only a few feet away, Ali Agca fired a gun several times, critically wounding the pope as four bullets struck his torso, right arm, and left hand. Ali Agca was immediately apprehended, and the gravely injured pope was rushed to the hospital. John Paul II would spend twenty-two days in the hospital recovering from Ali Agca's attack. In his first statement following the attempted assassination, John Paul requested that people "pray for my brother [Ali Agca], whom I have sincerely forgiven." And if you are inclined to casually dismiss this as just "what popes are supposed to do," may I suggest that until quite recently this is *not* how a pope would be expected to respond to an attempted murder.

Two years later, John Paul II visited Ali Agca in prison. In a private room the two men sat knee-to-knee, face-to-face, the pope holding the hand of his would-be-assassin...and forgiving him. Like the attempted assassination, this act of forgiveness was an event reported around the world.

There are two iconic photographic images that emerged from these two dramatic encounters of Pope John Paul II and Mehmet Ali Agca. The first is a photograph of the shocked face of Pope John Paul II, his papal robe splattered with blood, just after being shot. The second is a photograph of the shocked face of Mehmet Ali Agca as the pope met with him in prison and forgave him. In both pictures a shocked face seems to be asking the same question—"Why?"

Two iconic images. Two questioning faces. The first registering the shock of being the victim of unexpected and undeserved violence. The second registering the shock of being the recipient of unexpected and undeserved forgiveness. The second picture—the one of John Paul II forgiving a visibly shaken Ali Agca—was on the cover of the January 9, 1984 issue of *TIME* magazine, with the caption "Why Forgive?" Why indeed? The pope's whispered words of pardon to his would-be assassin were a clarion shout to the world: *This is what Jesus looks like! This is what Christianity is! This is what Christians do!*

Over the next twenty years the pope not only befriended Ali Agca but Agca's family as well. When Ali Agca was released from prison in 2006, he held aloft a copy of the famous *TIME* magazine and called the man he had tried to murder his friend. I cannot think of a better contemporary example of a Christian imitating Christ than the pope's forgiveness of Ali Agca.

Christian recording artist Steve Taylor wrote a song about Pope John Paul II and Mehmet Ali Agca, which addresses the question posed on the cover of *TIME* magazine—"Why Forgive?"

> I saw a man
> He was holding the hand
> That had fired a gun at his heart...
>
> I saw the eyes
> And the look of surprise
> As he left an indelible mark...
>
> Follow his lead
> Let the madness recede
> When we shatter the cycle of pain...
>
> Come find release
> Go make your peace
>
> I saw a man
> With a hole in his hand
> Who could offer the miracle cure...
>
> Oh, will we live
> To forgive?[3]

Oh, will we live to forgive? That may be the most challenging question faced by followers of Christ. Jesus prayed for his tormentors to be forgiven when he could have called upon angels of vengeance. Stephen prayed for his executioners to be forgiven instead of calling out for revenge and payback as Matthathias had done. Pope John Paul II offered pardon as he held the hand of the man who had fired a gun at his heart. These are Christ and his imitators—ancient and modern. To follow their lead and let the madness recede and shatter the cycle of pain are what it means to bring Christian forgiveness into a world obsessed with revenge.

Who Is Your Ali Agca?

In another time, a pope who was attacked by a Muslim fanatic would have responded with his own form of violence, which in all likelihood would have escalated into a Christian holy war and Islamic jihad. Violence would have won. Vengeance would have won. Satan would have won. But Pope John Paul II did not respond to violence with violence, vengeance with vengeance, satanic ways with satanic ways. Instead he imitated Christ, took the blow, loved his enemy, forgave his assailant, overcame evil with good, and turned the ugliness of religiously inspired violence into the beauty of Christlike forgiveness.

In his hatred, Ali Agca fired bullets of hate into the body of John Paul II, and though the bullets almost took the pope's life, the hate never touched his soul. John Paul II responded with whispered words of love and forgiveness—words that lodged in the soul of Ali Agca. Those words seem to have transformed this troubled man. They certainly caused multitudes around the world to ponder the possibilities of forgiveness.

So here is my question for you. Who is your Ali Agca? Who has fired the gun of hate at your heart? Hopefully you've not been shot with real bullets, but who hasn't been shot in the heart with hateful words—words that have the potential to poison your mind and ruin your soul? Will you escalate the violence and perpetuate the cycle of revenge, either in action or attitude, or will you imitate Christ and Stephen and John Paul II? Will you absorb the blow, forgive the perpetrator, and end the cycle of revenge? No, it's not easy. In fact, it may be the most difficult thing we are called to do in following Christ. But it may also be the most accurate way we imitate Christ and become genuinely Christlike—which is what it means to be Christian.

> *Who is your Ali Agca? Will you escalate the violence and perpetuate the cycle of revenge, either in action or attitude, or will you absorb the blow, forgive the perpetrator, and end the cycle of revenge?*

You can become *a* Christian in a moment. But to become Christian is another matter. In our evangelical churches we are very adept at teaching people how to become *a* Christian—how to receive the forgiveness available in Christ. We have not been nearly so adept at teaching people how to become Christian— how to become Christlike in a way that helps flood a world hell-bent on vengeance with the grace of forgiveness. But as you read the New Testament, you will find that Christ and his apostles place far more emphasis on becoming Christian than on becoming *a* Christian.

I fear we have contented ourselves with the self-congratulation of becoming *a* Christian, when the call of discipleship is to become Christian, to become Christlike, to become imitators of Christ in a fallen world where true imitation of Christ is radically counter-cultural and deeply counterintuitive. To meet hate with hate, vengeance with vengeance, violence with violence is the way of the fallen world, the way of fallen angels, the way of fallen man. It's the way that seems right, but it always ends in death.*

The way of Christ is the way of the cross and radical mercy leading to eternal life. But in our unrenewed minds, we are endlessly attracted to the way of Judah the Hammer—the vigilante messiah. The way of Jesus the Lamb who lays down his life to absorb the blow and end the vicious cycle seems like suicidal acquiescence with evil—and it is, unless you believe in God's intervention through resurrection. This is why the cross of Christ is a scandal, that is, unless you believe in the vindication of the Resurrection. The apostle Paul understood this when he spoke of the offense of the cross in Galatians 5:11. The Greek word for offense is *skandalon* or scandal. Yes, there is a scandal to the cross.

> The Cross is a scandal on every level
> A king with a crown of thorns
> A death march processional
> Acclamation by insult
> It's a macabre coronation.
>
> The Cross is a scandal on every level
> You say he won a war?
> You can't win a war that way
> You have to kill to win a war
> Who could win a war that way?
>
> The Cross is a scandal on every level
> Love your enemy
> Forgive your enemy

---

* Proverbs 14:12

Reconcile your enemy
Whoever heard such madness?

The Cross is a scandal on every level
"Take up your cross and follow me"
Who would ever sign up for that?
Promise me pleasure and riches
Don't bid me come and die.

The Cross is a scandal on every level
We long for glory and we're given this
We look for a kingdom and we get that
The glorious kingdom of a crucified king?
We want gold and silver, success and splendor.

The Cross is a scandal on every level
Pharaoh did it first
Alexander did it great
Caesar did it best
But not a crucified conqueror.

The Cross is a scandal on every level
Give us sword and shield
Something we can win with
Not outstretched arms
And a pierced side.

The Cross is a scandal on every level
No wonder the followers fled
What was there left to follow?
It's the ultimate dead end
It's common sense to run from that.

The Cross is a scandal on every level
You say it's the road that leads to life?

> Quite obviously it's the way of death
> And when you're dead the story ends
> Unless you believe what the silly women said.[4]

To believe the resurrection report of the "silly women" is to believe the Christian gospel. It's also how you become *a* Christian. But to imitate Christ in his radical version of crucified love and costly forgiveness is how you become Christian. To believe in the resurrection of the crucified Messiah is how you become *a* Christian—to take up your cross and imitate the crucified Messiah is how you become Christian. Don't let the indefinite article *a* prevent you from embarking upon the difficult journey of becoming Christian and truly Christlike. The call of disciple-ship is to become Christian—Christian not as status, but as the imitation of Christ.

So again I ask you, who is your Ali Agca? Who is the person who has fired the gun of hateful words (or worse) at your heart? A former friend? A coworker? An ex-spouse? A true enemy? And what have you done with your Ali Agca? Perhaps he or she has been locked up in your personal prison of resentment, your dungeon of private punishment. Will you dare to imitate Pope John Paul II, who imitated Christ? Will you go to your Ali Agca and dare to whisper words of pardon? Or will you keep Ali Agca locked up tight until you have exacted the last penny of your revenge?

Matters of Injustice

In Matthew 18, Jesus tells the memorable parable of a servant who owed his master the fantastically absurd amount of ten thousand talents—an amount equivalent to ten thousand years of servant wages. A debt so enormous it would take at least two hundred lifetimes to repay! As the indebted servant and his family were about to be sold into slavery, he fell to his knees and begged for patience and time to repay. How much time? Perhaps two hundred years? In response, the benevolent master forgave the servant his entire debt.

But instead of being transformed into a generous and forgiving person through his encounter with extravagant mercy, the servant went out and found a fellow servant who owed him a hundred denarii (equivalent to a hundred days of wages). That is, of course, far from an insignificant amount, but nothing in comparison to the ten thousand talents he had been forgiven. He took his debtor by the throat and demanded immediate payment. When his fellow servant was unable to pay, he had him thrown into prison. When the master heard of his atrocious behavior, he summoned the servant, called him *wicked*, and said this: "I forgave you all that debt because you pleaded with me. And should not you have had mercy on your fellow servant, as I had mercy on you?"* The master then had the ungrateful servant turned over to the jailers until he repaid all his debt. Jesus closes the parable with these chilling words: "So also my heavenly Father will do to every one of you, if you do not forgive your brother from your heart."†

In matters of injustice, we tend to fall into the trap of a false dichotomy. We tend to think that there are only two options: payment or punishment. The perpetrator of injustice must be made to pay, and if they can't pay, then they must be punished. Payment or punishment. Or, as Rachel Tulloch calls it, reparation or retribution.[5] This was the false dichotomy of the servant in Jesus's parable. When a fellow servant was discovered in his debt, he first demanded payment, and when payment was not possible, he insisted upon punishment. And yet this wicked servant (that is what Jesus calls him) should have known there was another option: pardon. He should have known of the

---

*   Matthew 18:32–33

†   Matthew 18:35

pardon option *because he had been a recipient of extravagant forgiveness.*

To be the recipient of God's extravagant forgiveness in Christ Jesus places an obligation upon the recipient to become the kind of person who embraces the third option, which is neither payment nor punishment—the option of pardon. But this is not a cheap pardon. There is real loss. In Jesus's parable, the master was willing to lose the unimaginable amount of ten thousand talents in order to pardon and keep the servant a free man. The master in effect said, "I will suffer the loss, I will bear the pain, in order that you can remain a free man in the human community." But his loss was substantial. And lest this be misunderstood as the offer of *cheap grace,* we must be reminded that at the center of God's offer of pardon stands the cross of Christ.

But let's understand the cross of Christ correctly. The cross of Christ is less the payment of a debt than it is the absorption of injustice. In the parable, the master is not repaid; he simply absorbs the loss. It is only through absorbing the pain of his loss that he is able to offer pardon to the debtor. Indeed, the forgiveness of great wrongs is never cheap but always painful, because someone must bear the loss. But when the pardoned servant imprisoned his fellow servant because he was unable to pay, he exited the world of grace and reentered the world of retribution where every penny has to be accounted for and every debtor must pay or be punished. In his lust for payback, he had broken the law of reciprocal grace set forth in the Lord's Prayer: "Forgive us our debts, as we also have forgiven our debtors."* In reverting to the dichotomy of payback or punishment, he had cast himself back into the torturous world of recycled revenge.

In her essay on "The Pain of Forgiveness," Rachel Tulloch

---

* Matthew 6:12

dispels the false dichotomy of reparation or retribution as well as the deterioration of forgiveness into cheap grace.

> Justice can never be achieved by reparation or retribution alone because like the servants' debts, true wrongs can never be repaid. The hurt and pain caused are not reversible. Punishing the guilty person does not undo the hurt either, even if it brings brief satisfaction to the victim, just as the first servant did not get his money back simply because the other man was in jail. Justice must be about much more than balancing out the wrongs of the world. It must be about making things *right*, about the kind of restoration that does not reverse the pain, but moves beyond it toward something new. And just as wrongs cannot be erased by punishment or repayment, they cannot really be erased by simple forgiveness either. When the master forgives the servant's debt, the debt does not simply disappear. *The master takes the loss!* He accepts the full brunt of the debt himself.[6]

Rachel Tulloch's vision of forgiveness is not a magical way of balancing the scales, but a way to move beyond the score-keeping of the scales *toward something new*. If we really want to live in God's new world, we have to be willing to suffer the pain of costly forgiveness, for only then can we experience the world where all things are made new. There is nothing older then the cycle of revenge—the keeping and settling of scores. It takes the born-again eyes that belong to the new creation to fully appreciate that a world where you make your debtors pay their debts is the world where you will be made to pay your debts. What the world needs if it is to move beyond the endless cycle of revenge is a Jubilee—a Jubilee of reciprocal and costly forgiveness.

At the end of the parable, Jesus says to us, "You must forgive your brother from your heart."* And if we don't, Jesus makes it clear that we have excluded ourselves from the generous realm of God's mercy. In the case of John Paul II and Ali Agca, the pope could forgive Ali Agca from his heart, though Ali Agca would still be subject to prosecution by the civil authorities for his crime. The pope's choice to forgive or not to forgive had an indirect effect upon Ali Agca, but it had a very direct effect upon his own spiritual condition—his own capacity to receive the mercy of God. I'll have more to say about the relationship of forgiveness and justice later on, but for the Christ follower, the issue is the manner in which the heart responds to a suffered injustice.

> *Allowing forgiveness to purge the unforgiveness in our hearts is what enables us to move beyond injustice and not be chained to it for life.*

When we are a victim of injustice (or a perceived injustice—and we must acknowledge that at times our perspective can be skewed), we are wounded. We have been shot in the heart by words and acts of hatred. The only way to remove the deadly bullet from our heart is through forgiveness. This is how you prevent yourself from becoming a victim twice over—first as a victim of injustice, then as a victim of systemic bitterness. The doctors were able to remove the bullets fired from Ali Agca's gun, but only John Paul II could prevent Ali Agca's hate from lodging in his soul. And the hatred could only be extracted by forgiveness.

John Paul II went to the prison to visit and forgive Ali

---

* Matthew 18:35

Agca so that his own soul would not become imprisoned. John Paul II could not prevent Ali Agca's attack upon his person, but he could prevent Ali Agca's hatred from defining and ultimately deforming him. When you are the recipient of hate, there is always the danger that you will allow yourself to be defined and deformed by that hate. The only way of exorcising the demon of hate is through the purgative of forgiveness. Allowing forgiveness to purge the unforgiveness in our hearts is what enables us to move beyond injustice and not be chained to it for life.

"I Don't Want to Forget, but I Want to Forgive"

Ingrid Betancourt was a French-Colombian senator when revolutionary terrorists kidnapped her in 2002. Before being rescued by Colombian security forces in 2008, she suffered deplorable treatment as a captive for six and a half years in the jungles of Colombia. For nearly the entire time of her captivity, she was chained to trees and other prisoners. Shortly after her rescue, Ingrid Betancourt appeared on the *Larry King Live* show. During the interview, King asked Betancourt if she held any bitterness toward her captors. Her reply was remarkable.

> I decided many years ago that when I was released I wouldn't take out of the jungle any kind of bitterness or any kind of eagerness to seek for revenge. I don't want to forget, but I want to forgive.[7]

I admire the courage and wisdom of Ingrid Betancourt. Having been freed from six and a half years of chains, she knew that without forgiveness she would remain chained to her jungle of injustice. The only way to really be free was through forgiveness. Forgiveness alone could break the chains. And yet there is her insightful remark about forgiveness and forgetting. "I don't want to forget, but I want to forgive." In those few words Ingrid Betancourt has touched on something very important in the realm of forgiveness. There is often a cheap naïveté about forgiveness that too easily equates forgiveness with forgetting—"forgive and forget," as the saying goes. And whereas I believe there are situations and ways in which forgetting may be a part of forgiveness, it needs to be stressed that Christian forgiveness does not call us to forget; it calls us to break the cycle of revenge. Forgiveness is not about a complete rejection of justice, but rather it involves the transfer of that justice to God. Again, I'll have more to say on the complicated relationship between justice and forgiveness later. But forgiveness is always possible, even if painful. Forgiveness is always possible, even when forgetting is either impossible or unwise.

Forgetting is not the same as forgiving. Amnesia is not the answer to a world stuck in the endless cycle of revenge. This is true for the simple reason that memory is an essential part of forming our identity. There are some things that occur in our lives that, if forgotten, would seriously lessen our authenticity. If certain events were forgotten entirely, we would quite simply not be fully ourselves. Jesus remembered his crucifixion and could show his wounds—his capacity to forgive did not require that he forget. If Stephen forgot his stoning or if John Paul II forgot he was shot, or if Ingrid Betancourt forgot that she was kidnapped for six and a half years, they would all be less themselves. Their suffering is integral to their identity.

Forgetting is not essential in forgiving because the memory of injustice does not require that we eternally lust for revenge. It is possible in the grace of God for all the pain of injustice to be removed while the scar of memory remains—not as a memory that causes the pain to be relived, but as a memory that forms identity and allows the story to move toward a happy ending even though the middle of the story contains undeniable pain. Jesus, Stephen, John Paul II, and Ingrid Betancourt will all remember these defining moments of their lives where they suffered injustice, but their choice to forgive has drawn out the sting and allowed them to move well beyond the reach of continued suffering.

The prophet Zechariah speaks of Messiah being pierced and wounded, and when questioned about his wounds, he responds by describing the still visible scars as "...the wounds I received in the house of my friends."* Christ carries the scars of crucifixion forever as the eternal memory of the cross. But he speaks of the scars not in the context of *enemies* but of *friends*. His scars remind him not of enmity but of friendship. In fact, it is around the wounds of Christ that our friendship with the Savior is formed.

Again I see John Paul II imitating Christ in this manner. For the rest of his life, John Paul II carried on his body the scars that he received from Ali Agca's gun. But from those wounds was forged a friendship. In the end, both John Paul II and Ali Agca referred to one another as *friends*. I like to imagine that if John Paul II were questioned about the scars, he might very well reply by saying, "Oh, that is where I was shot by my friend." I even wonder if in the resurrection, though John Paul II will have a glorified body free of all infirmity, he might continue to carry the scars he received from his friend Ali Agca as an ongoing imitation of Christ. Not scars that cause anyone (not even Ali Agca) to feel pain, but scars that tell a wonderful story of grace.

Yet this does not mean that we need to *try* to remember every injustice we have suffered. There are some things that legitimately can be forgotten without impinging upon our

---

* Zechariah 13:6

authenticity. When speaking of suffering injustice, it must be remembered that we are not always entirely innocent. There are many times when the hostility in a relationship that has led to hurtful words and events has sprung from mutual disrespect. Both sides have made their contribution to injustice. In a marriage, we call it a fight. But when forgiveness wins the day and the relationship is healed, it is encouraging to know that there is the very real possibility of both parties moving on together in love even beyond the realm of remembering. For them, memory would serve no redeeming purpose. We don't and can't remember everything. What we remember and what we forget are ways of restructuring our past and thereby forging our identities. To live well, there are things to remember and there are things to forget. A perfect memory does not make a perfect person. Sometimes forgiveness is the art of forgetting. But whether in forgetting or in remembering, forgiveness is always the imitation of Christ.

Les Misérables is Victor Hugo's best and most famous novel. It is an epic story whose entire plot is based upon the possibilities of forgiveness. As the book opens, the reader meets the central character, Jean Valjean. He is a convict who has just been released from nineteen years of hard labor for "having broken a pane of glass and taken a loaf of bread" to feed his sister and her starving children. After walking four days, he arrives at a town where he is immediately recognized as a released convict. As a result, every inn and every home closes its doors to Jean Valjean. At one point Valjean walks past a church and angrily shakes his fist. As the exhausted man lies down upon a public bench tired, cold, and hungry, a kindly woman suggests that he knock on the door of the bishop's house.

Expecting to find the same rebuff from the bishop, Monseigneur Bienvenu (his name means *welcome!*), Valjean is surprised when the bishop welcomes him as an honored guest. The godly bishop tells Valjean, "You need not tell me who you are. This is not my house; it is the house of Christ." The bishop then tells Valjean he already knows his name—"Your name is my brother."

After serving his guest a hot meal, the bishop hands Valjean a silver candlestick to light his way and leads him to a bedroom where, for the first time in nineteen years, Valjean will sleep in a bed. But Valjean cannot sleep. He wrestles with temptation as he contemplates stealing the silver plates upon which dinner was served. Sadly, he gives in to temptation, steals the silver plates, and creeps off into the night.

The next morning when the silver plates are found missing, the bishop simply explains that all he has belongs to the poor, and if the poor have taken them, no crime has been committed. When Jean Valjean is apprehended and brought back to the Monseigneur Bienvenu's residence, the bishop shocks everyone when he says, "Ah, there you are! I am glad to see you. But I gave you the candlesticks also, which are silver like the rest, and would bring two hundred francs. Why did you not take them along with your plates?" As the police release the astounded Valjean, the Christlike bishop whispers to the former convict, saying, "Jean Valjean, my brother: you belong no longer to evil, but to good. It is your soul that I am buying for you. I withdraw it from dark thoughts and from the spirit of perdition, and I give it to God!"

Jean Valjean is saved. He is redeemed from evil; he is rescued from the spirit of perdition. In willing to be wronged, to suffer the loss, and to simply forgive, Monseigneur Bienvenu welcomes Jean Valjean from the cold world of exacting retribution into the warm hospitality of amazing grace. By an act of surprising mercy and undeserved forgiveness, Victor Hugo's Monseigneur Bienvenu becomes an imitation of Christ— the true Monseigneur (Lord) who welcomes sinners into the embrace of reconciliation. And Jean Valjean does receive that forgiveness, that salvation, and goes on to live a life committed to helping and forgiving others.

So as we consider the imitators of Christ—St. Stephen, John Paul II, Monseigneur Bienvenu—we realize how forgiveness can save a soul—and not only the soul of the offender, but also the soul of the offended. Forgiving injustice by suffering the loss without retaliation, and thus bringing the possibility of redemption to all involved, is the fullest imitation of Christ available to us.

4

NO FUTURE WITHOUT FORGIVENESS

OUR HAPPINESS LIES in hope. If we can approach the future with hope, we can be happy. This is because hope is the prevailing attitude that the pain and disappointments of the past do not have to be endlessly repeated. Hope dares to imagine the future as a legitimate alternative to the vicious repetitions of the past. But the refusal to forgive is a toxic memory that endlessly pulls the painful past into the present. The toxic memory of the unforgiven past poisons the present and contaminates the future. This toxic attitude is well represented by Solomon in the opening lines of his poem Ecclesiastes.

> Vanity of vanities, says the Preacher,
> vanity of vanities! All is vanity....
> What has been is what will be,
> and what has been done is what will be done,
> and there is nothing new under the sun.
>   —ECCLESIASTES 1:2, 9

All is vanity. The past must be repeated. The future holds nothing new. There is no hope. Fortunately, the cynicism of Solomon as a divine revelation of the futility of the life estranged from God is not the final word on the possibilities for the future found in Scripture. The prophets (especially Isaiah), the apostles, and, most importantly, Jesus all offer a radically different vision for the future. They don't speak of vanity, futility, and meaningless repetition, but of purpose, meaning, and the possibility of new beginnings. Yet the prophetic and apostolic vision of a hopeful future is predicated upon our willingness to follow Christ and untangle our lives from the past through the practice of forgiveness. For without the practice of Christlike forgiveness, the cynical poet is right—there is nothing new under the sun. Or as Archbishop Desmond Tutu has said, "There is no future without forgiveness."[1] Forgiveness is both closing the door on a painful past and opening a new door to look toward a hopeful future.

Forgiveness Frames Your Future

The Old Testament patriarch Joseph understood the necessity of forgiveness in closing the door on a painful past in order to open the door to a promising future. As we consider the role of forgiveness in framing our future according to hope, it may be helpful to briefly recall Joseph's remarkable story.

Joseph was a dreamer—the eleventh of twelve brothers. He was also the favorite of his father. The favoritism of his father, along with his dreamy optimism, caused his less favored and less visionary brothers to resent him deeply—a resentment deep enough that they could wish him dead. In the end they did not murder him, but they did something nearly as reprehensible: they sold him into slavery and reported him dead. All of this transpired when Joseph was but seventeen years old. For the next thirteen years Joseph lived the life of a slave in Egypt. At times he found favor with his superiors and began to rise from his lowly status. At other times he was maliciously vilified and suffered deep injustice. This went on for thirteen years. And thirteen years of unjust suffering is plenty of time to potentially build up a lot of resentment. But just when Joseph was at his lowest point, things suddenly changed, and his dreams finally began to come true. In a dramatic reversal of fortunes (certainly a prophetic prefiguring of the resurrection and ascension of Christ), the favored son, unjustly treated and counted as dead, was exalted by Pharaoh to rule over the empire of Egypt.

In a conventional tale of rags to riches and the inevitable triumph of the good guy, this is where the story would end and the credits would roll. But Joseph's story does *not* end here. Joseph's story does not end here because the story is not really about Joseph but about the whole family of Israel and their salvation. So the story continues until nine years later when Joseph is reunited with his brothers, who are on the verge of starvation and now completely in Joseph's power. Now the tables are turned. Now Joseph has the opportunity to exact his revenge. Now Joseph can have his brothers sold into slavery as they had sold him into slavery. But Joseph does not do this. Instead Joseph forgives his brothers, provides for their families, and saves the seed of Abraham. Forgiveness had provided Israel with a future.

Nevertheless, the guilt-racked brothers are still afraid of Joseph. They are convinced that though the day of Joseph's vengeance has been delayed, it is still surely to come. They cannot believe that Joseph could wield such power and not use it to exact justice in the form of revenge. They believe that Joseph is simply biding his time until their father is dead. So when their elderly father, Jacob, dies, they fear Joseph will at long last act in vengeance toward them. In their fear of impending retaliation they said, "Now Joseph will show his anger and pay us back for all the wrong we did to him."* Joseph's brothers lived in the ugly world of paybacks and reciprocal revenge. Now that their father was no longer around to restrain Joseph, they were certain that payback was coming.

The world of paybacks and reciprocal revenge is a world where the strong intimidate the weak and where fear is both a means of manipulating your enemy and the specter that haunts your own dark dreams. In the world of paybacks, the first order of business when gaining power is to exact revenge upon your enemies—to make them pay. In the world of paybacks, this is a primary motivation for seeking power in the first place—it's the power to get even. Had Joseph played according to the rules of payback, he and his brothers would have been stuck in a family feud and an endless cycle of revenge—a cycle they would have passed on to their descendants. A legacy of retaliation. An inheritance of reprisal. A bequest of bitterness. Sadly, the tradition of maintaining family, national, or ethnic "honor" through the practice of revenge is a tradition not only firmly entrenched in Middle East culture but also all too present in the whole world. In the world of vengeful payback, life becomes an endless cycle of revenge, retaliation, and retribution—a vicious circle of paybacks, getting even, and settling the score. Except that the score is never settled, and eventually the origin of the conflict is lost in the dust of history while the lust for endless revenge remains alive and well. This is how evil remains the top dog no matter who is in power, and justice becomes only a cheap word to justify mindless acts of revenge. The testimony of the wars and atrocities perpetrated under this system are what we blithely call "world history."

In the system of paybacks, Joseph and his brothers (the redemptive seed of Abraham!) will be stuck in a family feud of recycled revenge. Time will roll on, but nothing will change.

---

*   Genesis 50:15, NLT

There will be nothing new under the sun. Unless. Unless forgiveness can break the cycle and give them a future. Here is
where we see just how essential forgiveness is to God's program
of redemption, for without forgiveness the seed of Abraham has
no future, just endless repetitions of the painful past. Without
forgiveness, the seed of Abraham will never arrive at its redemptive destiny. But Joseph is smarter than that. Joseph is better
than that. Joseph is more Christlike than that. Joseph did not go
from a prisoner to a prince only to be imprisoned by the dead-
end cycle of revenge. So, to his brothers who are full of fear and
expecting a retaliatory payback, Joseph says, "Don't be afraid of
me. Am I God, that I can punish you? You intended to harm me,
but God intended it all for good."*

These words come at the close of Genesis. It is only because
Joseph chose to forgive that the Bible has a future. Only because
Joseph chose to absorb the injustice, forgive his brothers, and
move forward by trusting God can God's project of redemption
through the seed of Abraham move forward. Without forgiveness, the Bible doesn't get past Genesis. Without forgiveness
there really is no future!

But there is a future, because Joseph chooses to forgive his
brothers. Yet Joseph's choice to forgive is no exercise in cheap
grace. Joseph does not say, "Oh, it was nothing." Because it
wasn't nothing. It was harm, it was evil, and it was injustice.
Joseph does not move forward in forgiveness by calling injustice justice or evil good. Joseph names what has been done
as wrong, but Joseph chooses to forgive by reconciling with
his brothers and entrusting the matter of justice to the hands
of God. In fact, Joseph can see how God is never bound by
evil and how God was even able to use the evil *that God did
not cause* to work toward a redemptive end. Joseph remembered the wrong that had been done to him—thirteen years

---

* Genesis 50:19–20, NLT

of slavery—but he did not remember it in a toxic manner that would poison the present and contaminate the future. Joseph had to remember the injustice he had suffered because it was so much a part of his story. But Joseph would remember in the context of forgiveness and not as fuel for vengeance. Joseph did not forgive and forget. Joseph forgave and remembered. But as Joseph remembered, he simultaneously released his brothers from their moral debt and freed the whole family to enter into reconciliation.

> *Without forgiveness, the Bible doesn't get past Genesis. Without forgiveness there really is no future!*

Another point worth noting from this story, which closes out the epic narrative of Genesis, is that this is the formal introduction in the Bible of the theme of forgiveness. It is at this point that the supremely important word *forgive* first walks onto the stage of Scripture. The first use of the word *forgive* in the Bible is when we read, "Please *forgive* your brothers for the great wrong they did to you."* This theme will be repeated throughout the long story the Bible tells. It will be a recurrent theme of the psalmists and prophets. It will be found in the Sermon on the Mount. It will be heard in the Lord's Prayer. It will be present at the cross. It will be present at the Resurrection. The apostles will take the message of forgiveness to the world. But it is here in Genesis, in the story of Joseph and his brothers, that we are first requested to "please forgive your brothers."

---

* Genesis 50:17, NLT, emphasis added

Genesis comes to a close recounting the four-thousand-year-old story of a prisoner who becomes president and gives a nation a future based on forgiveness. But it's not a story that must be relegated to ancient history. These things still happen. Injustices still occur, and occasionally great souls still rise up to lead people out of the dead end of retaliation into a future only reconciliation can create. The story of a prisoner who becomes president and gives his people a future based on forgiveness is the story of the Hebrew patriarch Joseph. It's also the story of Nelson Mandela.

Restorative Justice

The history of South Africa is one of the saddest stories in the shameful saga of European colonialism. Before the story of South Africa would give rise to hope, it would first give rise to a racist regime that lasted until the final decade of the twentieth century. In 1948, after centuries of colonial exploitation, the all-white Afrikaaner National Party instituted a government policy of segregation and discrimination based on race—a system that legally extended and institutionalized the already long-existing practices of racism. The system was known as *apartheid*– a Dutch word meaning "separateness." (Interestingly, the words *apartheid* and *Pharisee* both mean the same thing!)

Under apartheid, only whites—approximately 10 percent of the South African population[2]—had the right to vote. Businesses, beaches, bridges, restaurants, theaters, hospitals, and even ambulances were designated "Whites Only." As part of apartheid's brutal practices, six hundred thousand non-whites were forcibly removed and relocated in order to enlarge "Whites Only" territory. The whole system of apartheid was designed to impoverish the black majority and enrich the white minority. Protests against racial inequality were violently crushed. Antiapartheid activists were arrested. A typical punishment for antiapartheid activism was public whipping. During the years of apartheid, thousands of blacks were *legally* subjected to the dehumanizing practice of public whipping. Others were jailed. Others were tortured. Others simply disappeared. And through it all, the whites-only Dutch Reformed Church of South Africa assured their members that apartheid was certainly God's will. But the wider world knew better, and eventually internal activism, international condemnation, and economic sanctions made apartheid untenable. In 1994, the apartheid regime was dismantled, and nonwhite South Africans were at last given the right to vote.

The end of apartheid and the emergence of democracy in South Africa opened the door for Nelson Mandela to step onto the world stage. In 1964, at the age of forty-six, Mandela had been sentenced to life in prison as an antiapartheid activist with the African National Congress (ANC). Released in 1990 after twenty-seven years of hard labor in a rock quarry that nearly ruined his eyesight, Nelson Mandela became the leader of the ANC. Following his release from prison, Nelson Mandela made a deliberate choice to reenter the South African struggle without bitterness and diligently worked with President F. W. de Klerk for a peaceful transition to a democratic government. In 1993, Mandela and de Klerk were awarded the Nobel Peace Prize. A year later, South Africa held their first full and free democratic elections. Nelson Mandela had waited seventy-six years before he could vote, and now his fellow countrymen elected him the first president of the new South Africa. The prisoner had become president. Joseph's amazing story had been repeated. And if there was any question as to whether President Mandela would pursue a course of reconciliation or revenge, the answer was given when he invited his white jailer to be his honored guest at his presidential inauguration.

But what would the future hold for South Africa? Many assumed there would be a bloodbath of retaliation. Many assumed that now it would be time for those who had so long been denied justice to exact their revenge with violent retribution. But that didn't happen. South Africa instead made a peaceful transition from a racist regime to a stable democracy. It was nothing short of a miracle. But how was this accomplished? It was accomplished through prophetic imagination—through daring to imagine a new and creative way of moving beyond the wrongs of the past. Not the way of exacting revenge and not the way of ignoring justice, but by the way of restorative justice—a new way that gave room for both truth and reconciliation. Nelson Mandela understood that trials similar to the Nazi war crimes trials following World War II would rip South Africa apart. He also knew that to simply forget the injustices of the past would be a further injustice—an injustice to the truth. Instead, Nelson Mandela envisioned a third way. Not Nuremburg trials, not national amnesia, but restorative justice.

To lead the nation beyond the toxic memories of the past, which had the capacity to poison the future, *but to do it in a way that did not sacrifice the truth*, Nelson Mandela established the Truth and Reconciliation Commission. To lead this radical new approach to addressing injustice, President Mandela appointed Anglican archbishop and fellow Nobel Peace Prize laureate Desmond Tutu as chairman of the Truth and Reconciliation Commission. And it was Bishop Tutu who gave the world the wonderful phrase, "There is no future without forgiveness."

Here is the brilliance and beauty, the wisdom and grace, the imagination and creativity of the Truth and Reconciliation Commission. If any person who had committed crimes under the apartheid system would make a full and public confession before the commission, they could immediately receive full amnesty for their crimes. (Unconfessed apartheid crimes remained subject to conventional criminal prosecution.) And what was the result? More than seven thousand people made their confession and applied for amnesty, although not all received it.[3] Many of the amnesty hearings were conducted in churches. I cannot imagine a more appropriate place for truth and reconciliation to prevail and for amnesty to be given than in a church.

> *The way of forgiveness does not forget the past, but through truth and reconciliation it finds a way beyond toxic memory. It is the way of restorative justice.*

Another aspect of the Truth and Reconciliation project was the opportunity for victims to tell their stories—to tell the nation and the world what had been done to them in the name of apartheid. Their stories were broadcast on television and radio and printed in the newspapers. More than twenty thousand victims came forward to tell their story.[4] As they did so, they gave truth the hearing it had so long been denied. Sin was named and shamed, and truth had its day. In this way, justice did not become ugly retribution, which would simply set the table for the next cycle of revenge. But neither was justice denied and victims forgotten. A third way had been found. The way of truth. The way of reconciliation. The way of forgiveness. The way that could give a nation a future beyond the self-destruction of forever seeking revenge. Truth and reconciliation had danced together, and neither was denied. Or, as the psalmist said, "Mercy and truth have met together; righteousness and peace have kissed."*

The way of forgiveness does not forget the past, but through truth and reconciliation it finds a way beyond toxic

---

*   Psalm 85:10, NKJV

memory. It is the way of restorative justice. In his book *No Future Without Forgiveness*, Desmond Tutu describes restorative justice like this.

> We contend that there is another kind of justice, *restorative justice*....Here the central concern is not retribution or punishment.... [T]he central concern is the healing of breaches, the redressing of imbalances, the restoration of broken relationships, a seeking to rehabilitate both the victim and the perpetrator, who should be given the opportunity to be reintegrated into the community he has injured by his offense.... Thus we would claim that justice, restorative justice, is being served when efforts are being made to work for healing, for forgiving, and for reconciliation.[5]

Nelson Mandela and Desmond Tutu found a way to live the Lord's Prayer on a national level. A nation was praying, "Forgive us our trespasses as we forgive those who trespass against us." A nation was praying, "Thy kingdom come, Thy will be done, on earth as it is in heaven." And in a very real way (if certainly incomplete) the kingdom of God was breaking in among men, and through the Jesus way of forgiveness a nation was given a future it could have no other way. This is what Amos dreamed of when he spoke of justice rolling down like water.[*] This is, at least in part, what Jesus intended when he spoke of making disciples of the nations.[†] Restorative justice is the kind of justice the prophets talked about. This is the kind of justice Jesus wants to bring to a broken world. This is the kind of justice that can happen when we choose to end the cycle of revenge. This is the kind of justice that can happen when we are more interested in restoration than retaliation.

---

[*]   Amos 5:24
[†]   Matthew 28:19

"God Meant It for Good"

The German philosopher Friedrich Nietzsche was something of a mad prophet—a mad, bound-for-the-outer-darkness, Balaam-like prophet, but prophetic nonetheless. Nietzsche got a lot wrong, but he got a lot right too. In *Thus Spake Zarathustra*, Nietzsche makes a very profound observation concerning the past and redemption when he says, "To redeem what is past...that only do I call redemption!"[6] For redemption to be complete and honestly give us a hopeful future, it must be able to address and in some way redeem the past. Through the act of forgiveness the past is not forgotten, but by faith in God's redemptive work it comes to be viewed in a new way. The injustice is to be remembered, but it is not allowed to poison the present and dictate the future. Forgiveness, when done as an expression of faith in God, allows us to have a new and redemptive perspective on the past. After Joseph was reconciled with his brothers through forgiveness, he could look back upon his bitter past with a new perspective: "As for you, you meant evil against me, but God meant it for good, to bring it about that many people should be kept alive, as they are today."* For Joseph, the past had been redeemed through forgiveness. But this redemptive perspective upon the past can only be obtained by faith. We must be able to believe that God is at work in our act of forgiveness. And we must believe that God is so deeply at work in redemption as to in some way redeem the past and thus free the future to be something more than a tragic repetition of the past.

In the ancient story of the Jewish patriarch Joseph, we see how forgiveness gave the fledgling nation of Israel a future beyond a family feud. In the modern story of Nelson Mandela and Desmond Tutu, we see how two national fathers made room for forgiveness and gave South Africa a future beyond

---

* Genesis 50:20

the cycle of revenge. Joseph moved Israel beyond the cruelty of fraternal betrayal. South Africa moved beyond the cruelty of racist apartheid. And from wise men ancient and modern, we seek to learn the lesson—a lesson to which the whole canon of Scripture bears ample witness: there is no future without forgiveness.

So what is your story? Who has been cruel to you? Perhaps bitterly cruel. What injustice have you suffered? How have you been mistreated? Perhaps miserably so. Who has cheated you? Abused you? Mistreated you? Lied to you? Lied *about* you? Maybe it was last week. Maybe it was a lifetime ago. As you remember your suffered injustice, how does it affect the way you view the future? Or let me put it another way: What are you waiting for? Are you waiting to get even? A chance for payback? An opportunity to exact your revenge? If so, you have no future.

You may get even, you may achieve payback, you may gain your revenge, *but you will stay forever chained to the injustice done to you.* You are in danger of forming your identity around your injustice in such a way that it forever shapes your future. Even if you get even, you will still drag that ball and chain with you. In looking for an opportunity to be cruel to the person who was cruel to you, you will become a cruel person. And in becoming a cruel person, your cruelty will, in all likelihood, not be limited to the person or persons who have treated you cruelly. In seeking the opportunity to repay cruelty with cruelty, cruelty will become your identity, your lifestyle, and your character. Tragically, you will do the very thing you hate: you will inflict cruel injustice upon others.

Worse yet, you will *become* the very thing you hate. This is how evil perpetuates itself. This is how evil moves from host to host until the whole world lies in the power of the evil one.* Evil is only defeated when someone absorbs the blow and forgives, thus ending the cycle of evil. Absorbing the blow without retaliation *by exercising the option to forgive* is not weakness or acquiescence with injustice; it is taking up your cross and following Jesus. It is following Jesus to Calvary, and there ending evil through the triumph of forgiveness. Forgiveness is not weakness; it is the power of God—the power of God to overcome evil by depriving evil of a host for retaliation.

Forgiveness—Abandoning the Devil's Game

Again, it needs to be restated, you don't have to forget the past. Forgiveness is not amnesia. You don't have to say you weren't wronged. Forgiveness is found in truth and not a lie. You can remember the wrong. It can be named and shamed as a sin. You don't have to abandon the hope of justice. Justice is a passion of the Lord. "For the LORD loves justice; he will not forsake his saints."† Because you believe in God's passion for justice, you can leave justice in the hands of God. The call to forgiveness is not to forget the past. The call to forgiveness is not a form of self-deception. The call to forgiveness is not an abandonment of justice. The call to forgiveness is the call to stop the cycle of revenge. The call to forgiveness is the call to abandon the devil's game. The call to forgiveness is the call to no longer collaborate with death.

British alternative rock band Coldplay has sold more than fifty million albums worldwide. Their best-selling album is the Grammy Award–winning *Viva la Vida* or *Death and All His Friends*. In the song "Death and All His Friends" Chris Martin sings:

---

*   1 John 5:19

†   Psalm 37:28

No, I don't want a battle from beginning to end
I don't want a cycle of recycled revenge
I don't want to follow death and all of his friends.[7]

I love that lyric. This is exactly the attitude Christians are to adopt in heeding Jesus's call to a life of radical forgiveness. We are the followers of the one who taught us to pray, "Forgive us our debts as we forgive our debtors," and who cried from the cross, "Father, forgive them," and who said, "If you forgive the sins of any, they are forgiven." To follow Jesus is to *not* follow death and all his friends—friends like revenge, retribution, and retaliation. The friends of death are a vicious lot—inflicting paybacks, getting even, settling the score. The friends of death are the things that bring the most misery to our world—things like bitterness, hatred, and war. Through adopting the call of Jesus to employ radical forgiveness, we find a way out of the cycle of recycled revenge. We find a way out of a futile life that is nothing more than a battle from beginning to end.

> Forgiveness is not weakness; it is the power
> of God—the power of God to overcome evil
> by depriving evil of a host for retaliation.

This is the Jesus way. And we need to see that the Jesus way is far more than "how to go to heaven when you die." When Jesus said he was the way, the truth, and the life,* he wasn't just saying he was the way to salvation in a postmortem afterlife; rather he was claiming that his way of living is the true way that leads to life. The Jesus way is always the way of forgiveness. Seventy times seven! This is the way that ends the

---

* John 14:6

endless battle, that breaks the cycle of recycled revenge, and that refuses to follow death and all of his friends. This is the way that gives the future a hope.

But we will not casually glide into this way of radical forgiveness. You can be quite certain of that. The Jesus way of forgiveness, the way that gives hope to the future, is decidedly *not* the way of the world. The way of the world has always been the bloody and violent way of getting even and passing on to the next generation a reason to hate. This is what has filled the world with darkness and made the study of world history little more than the study of war. And this is why the prophetic hope has always been for a way out of the darkness into a day when we would study war no more.* To claim that Jesus is the Savior of the world without addressing recycled revenge and the wars it creates—from personal and petty to global and catastrophic—is to fall into the Gnostic trap of reducing the Savior *of* the world into a savior *from* the world. Jesus came to save the world, not save us from the world. The difference is immense.

The sense in which Jesus saves us *from* the world is the way in which he saves us from the futile ways of the fallen world order. And nothing is more central to the fallen world order than the law of self-preservation through vengeful retaliation. This is what prevents the world from having a future that is little more than a technologically advanced repetition of the bloody past. Consider how we have advanced...while nothing has changed. Instead of retaliating against our enemies one at a time with sticks and stones, we can now retaliate against a hundred thousand at a time with nuclear bombs. This is what we call "progress." We are kidding ourselves if we think the world has advanced simply because our technology has advanced. Unless we find a way out of the darkness of endless

---

* Isaiah 2:4; Micah 4:3

revenge, our advanced technology only leads us further and faster into the black abyss of self-destruction.

Jesus constantly insisted that he came to teach the world a new way and that this new way was the way of his Father who had sent him. The world had lost its way in the darkness of estrangement from God and alienation from neighbor. Lost in this loveless darkness, the world knew only how to lash out in retaliation at everyone perceived as an enemy—the hated *them*. In this dark world, it was all too easy for Satan to manipulate clans and tribes and nations until the majority of *others* belonged to the hated *them*. In such a world, feud, quarrel, conflict, and war are the inevitable results. This is the way in which there is truly no future, only the dead end of bitter reprisal. The same as it ever was.

In this kind of *lostness*, technological advancement only exacerbates the problem. No sooner does technology advance than we invent a way to use it against our enemies—whether it's how to forge bronze or harness the atom. This is why the Son of God came—to give us a way out of the darkness. He claimed that whoever believed in him and his teaching would find the way out of the loveless darkness and would learn to live in the light. According to Jesus, to live in the light is to actually live the radical precepts that he taught.*

Embrace the Way of the Cross

I'm convinced that one of the reasons we are so deeply tempted to reduce the salvation found in Jesus Christ to a largely private and primarily postmortem event is that whereas we believe in Jesus as our "personal Savior," we are still not convinced of his ideas. At times we remain as cynical as Pilate. Sure, we believe that Jesus can save us for the next life, but in this life it is not the cross that saves, but the sword. Or so we think. But the sword of

---

* See John 12:44–50.

vengeance (and that's what we always claim the sword is for—the vengeance of justice) is the perfect symbol of a world stuck in the bitter cycle of revenge.

> *It's when Jesus embraces the cross and cries from the cross, "Father, forgive them for they know not what they do," that the world is given a future.*

No wonder when Pilate encountered Jesus on his way to the cross he could dismiss Jesus's claim that he had come into the world to bear witness to the truth with the cynical aphorism, "What is truth?"* For Pilate, truth was a captive to whatever was politically expedient. Pilate was a cynical and pragmatic politician. Pilate simply had no imagination. He could not imagine there was any other way to live than by being on the winning side of the sword of vengeance. But Jesus could. And did. This is why the Christian symbol is not a sword but the cross. And why the cross? Because *this* is how the world is changed. This is how the world is saved. This is how the world can move beyond the bitter cycle of revenge. This is how the world is given a future. It's when Jesus embraces the cross and cries from the cross, "Father, forgive them for they know not what they do," that the world is given a future. Yes, it is in this act that the world is given a future!

But do we believe it? Do we believe that the way of the cross, the way of absorbing the blow and the way of responding only with forgiveness, is the way that leads to a hopeful future? Do we believe that without forgiveness there is no future? Or are we too "practical" for that? By practical, I mean lacking in prophetic imagination...or perhaps just plain unbelieving. If

---

* See John 18:33-38.

so, we are far more like Pontius Pilate than we might like to admit. As Miroslav Volf has pointedly observed:

> Pilate deserves our sympathies, not because he was a good though tragically misunderstood man, but because we are not much better. We may believe in Jesus, but we do not believe in his ideas, at least not in his ideas about violence, truth, and justice.[8]

But we must believe. We must believe in Jesus—not only by believing in what the creeds confess concerning his identity—but by also believing in his *ideas*. Yes, we must dare to believe in Jesus's radical ideas of enemy-love and endless forgiveness, because without this kind of love and this kind of forgiveness, there is no future. The future you look for, the future you long for, the future that would free you from the unending repetition of the painful past, lies in your capacity to move beyond the past through the liberating practice of faith-based forgiveness. It is forgiveness that creates the future you want to live in.

5

FORGIVENESS THAT TRANSCENDS TRAGEDY

ORGIVENESS LIES AT the heart of God's project to set right
a world gone wrong. Ours is a gospel of forgiveness. A
gospel that is not to be confined to the stained-glass world
of sentimental piety, but a gospel intended for the healing of
the nations. Until forgiveness is embraced as part of the fundamental equation for redressing the ills of our world, we will
inevitably find ourselves enacting or endorsing the tired practice of violent retaliation, a practice that has caused human
history to be written in the genre of tragedy. God's solution
to the perpetuation of violence and vengeance is the startling
introduction of forgiveness.

Only forgiveness has the capacity to rescue human society
from the destructive vortex of violence and vengeance and give
us a healing alternative. Only forgiveness can create the world
of peace of which the prophets dared to dream. Forgiveness is
how God saves the sinner. The practice of forgiveness is how
God heals the world. Forgiveness is the miracle cure. Not the

cheap forgiveness that turns a blind eye to the reality of evil, but the costly forgiveness of the cross.

We who call ourselves Christians are recipients of the forgiveness that flows from the cross. But just as significantly, we are those called to be practitioners of Christlike forgiveness. We don't just partake of the forgiveness of the cross; we take up the cross. We too engage in the costly practice of radical forgiveness. We too pray in the midst of our pain, "Father, forgive them." In a broken world framed in revenge, we are to help flood creation with the healing grace of forgiveness. This is why forgiveness occupies center stage at all the most important places in the Christian faith: the Sermon on the Mount, the Lord's Prayer, Good Friday, Easter Sunday.

To be a Christian is to believe that saving forgiveness is found in the cross. But to be a Christian also means to take up the cross in a deliberate imitation of Jesus. Admittedly, Christ's call for us to take up our cross and follow him is filled with many implications, but the most obvious understanding of this call is that we are to emulate the way Jesus responded to evil as he hung upon the cross—by forgiving transgressors and refusing to be drawn into the cycle of revenge.

Historic Christianity has always understood that salvation comes from what Jesus did at his cross. But we must also understand that we are called to be ambassadors of that salvation by doing the same thing with our own cross. We too are to forgive the transgressors and refuse to be drawn into the cycle of revenge. I fully realize this is a Christianity more radical than most bargain for. But perhaps we need to be reminded that the fullness of salvation is not obtained at a bargain; it is obtained by taking up our cross and following Jesus.

Cheap Grace

The bane of the American church is consumer Christianity, comfortable Christianity, easy-cheesy-cotton-candy

Christianity, the low-grade Christianity of *what's in it for me?* This diluted Christianity offers a certain solace to the individual but is anemic before the principalities and powers of entrenched evil. If the essence of our Christianity affects only our Sunday mornings and our afterlife expectations, we are simply embracing a Christianized version of what is our true religion—the religion of self-preservation and self-promotion. This is the deceptive religion of the selfish individual and the arrogant empire. This is the religion that Dietrich Bonhoeffer called "cheap grace."

> Cheap grace is the deadly enemy of our Church....Cheap grace means grace sold on the market like cheapjacks' wares. The sacraments, the forgiveness of sin, and the consolations of religion are thrown away at cut prices....Grace without price; grace without cost!...Cheap grace means grace as a doctrine, a principle, a system....Grace alone does everything, they say, and so everything can remain as it was before....The world goes on the same old way....Cheap grace is the grace we bestow on ourselves....Cheap grace is grace without discipleship, grace without the cross.[1]

A cheap view of grace deceives us into thinking that nothing really has to change. Because we have "received Jesus as our personal Savior," we now possess our salvation and simply await our transfer to heaven by living a moderately Christianized version of the status quo. As the bumper-sticker theology goes, "Christians aren't perfect, *just forgiven*." But bumper stickers are a poor place to get your theology. We aren't *just forgiven*. We are forgiven that we might become practitioners of radical forgiveness. We are forgiven *forgivers*. Jesus does not offer his disciples the cheap grace of being *just forgiven*.

Instead, Jesus calls his disciples to an ethic of forgiveness and enemy-love that bears no resemblance to the ethic of individualism and empire that we see in the status quo. Compare the cheap grace of American bumper-sticker theology to the costly demands of discipleship, which Jesus sets forth in the Sermon on the Mount.

> You have heard that it was said, "You shall love your neighbor and hate your enemy." But I say to you, Love your enemies and pray for those who persecute you, so that you may be sons of your Father who is in heaven. For he makes his sun rise on the evil and on the good, and sends rain on the just and on the unjust. For if you love those who love you, what reward do you have? Do not even the tax collectors do the same? And if you greet only your brothers, what more are you doing than others? Do not even the Gentiles do the same? *You therefore must be perfect, as your heavenly Father is perfect.*
>
> —MATTHEW 5:43–48, EMPHASIS ADDED

So much for the "not perfect, just forgiven" bumper-sticker theology of cheap grace. Jesus calls us to a perfect imitation of our Father in heaven. Jesus links this to how we treat our enemies, how we relate to those who are genuinely evil. If we surrender to the status quo by loving our neighbors and hating our enemies, by praying for our friends and hating our adversaries, by blessing the good guys and hating the bad guys, we are refusing to bear the image of our Father—we are refusing to live as his sons and daughters. Returning good for good and evil for evil is the way the world has always operated. And it is why the world remains a violent and angry place. Jesus calls us to become sons and daughters of our Father in heaven through a mature imitation of God's love and kindness—a love and kindness that are extended to friend and foe, good and bad alike.

It will be helpful to keep in mind that Jesus did not present his ethic of enemy-love in the quiet and safe confines of American suburbia. Jesus lived in a violent world where his homeland was occupied by foreign troops. When Jesus was a small child, an armed Jewish revolt against the Roman occupiers broke out in Sepphoris—an important Galilean city just four miles from Nazareth (often considered to be the "city set upon a hill"). The Roman general Varus brutally crushed the rebellion and lined the road to Sepphoris with *two thousand* crucified Galilean rebels. "The grisly scene of human remains nailed to crosses lining the roadways was part of Rome's psychological warfare, a deterrent to future protestors."[2]

> *If we surrender to the status quo by loving our neighbors and hating our enemies, by praying for our friends and hating our adversaries, by blessing the good guys and hating the bad guys, we are refusing to bear the image of our Father— we are refusing to live as his sons and daughters.*

It's impossible to imagine that events like this did not have an enormous impact upon the young Jesus. The mass crucifixion of the rebels of Sepphoris undoubtedly shaped Jesus's concept of words like *cross* and *enemy*. We speak of *taking up the cross* in a world where virtually no one has seen a real crucifixion. Jesus spoke of taking up the cross in a world where crucifixions were all too common. And Jesus spoke of enemy-love where real and potentially violent enemies were as present as the nearest Roman garrison. The historical context of Jesus's Sermon on the Mount makes his words all the more astonishing. Jesus and his hearers knew about real crosses and real enemies.

Canadian theologian and pastor Brad Jersak reminds us, "Christ's teachings and Christ's death on the Cross are not two separate issues. Christ's *way*, the narrow path, is the road of loving and forgiving even unto death. And he didn't say, 'Let me do that for you.' He said, 'Come die with me.'"[3]

We turn the gospel into cheap grace when we think of the cross only in terms of what Jesus has done for us. The cross is also *the way* we are called to follow—the way of endless enemy-love. An honest reading of the Gospels makes an offer of cheap grace impossible. We too are called to love our enemies. We too are called to forgive our transgressors. The bully who has made your life a living hell. The ex-husband who betrayed you. The ex-wife who left you a lonely man. The backstabber who sabotaged your career. The criminal who violated your security. The abuser who violated your dignity. The activist who advocates everything you oppose. And on it goes. We are called to love, forgive, and bless these enemies. The consumer Christianity of self-preservation and self-promotion will never be able to meet the challenge of taking up the cross and forgiving an enemy.

Radical Grace...Amish Grace

From time to time we hear a story that reminds us there really are people who dare to live the life of radical forgiveness. The book *Amish Grace* tells such a story and opens with these words.

> *Amish. School. Shooting.* Never did we imagine that these words would appear together. But the unimaginable turned real on October 2, 2006, when Charles Carl Roberts IV carried his guns and his rage into an Amish schoolhouse near Nickel Mines, Pennsylvania.

Five schoolgirls died that day, and five others were seriously wounded. Turning a tranquil schoolhouse into a house of horror...[4]

Sadly, America has grown somewhat jaded to the news of school shootings. Unfortunately, it's what we've come to expect. But not in the quiet Amish countryside of rural Pennsylvania. This time we were again shocked and horrified. How could the blood of violence and murder stain the floor of an Amish schoolhouse?

Charles Roberts was a thirty-two-year-old dairy truck driver in Lancaster County, Pennsylvania. He and his wife, Amy, had three young children. The family attended church. But Roberts was a deeply embittered man. Nine years earlier their firstborn child, a daughter, had died twenty minutes after her birth. Of course, Charles and Amy grieved. Nevertheless, Charles Roberts could have had a good life with his loving wife and their three children; he instead allowed bitterness over the death of his daughter to consume him and turn him into a monster...a ticking time bomb.

In his suicide note, Roberts also confessed to having sexually molested two young relatives when he was twelve (though the relatives had no recollection of this event). The combination of shame and rage became a deadly toxin in his soul. Roberts was angry with God, angry with life, and angry with himself. In his mind, someone had to pay. Payback was the foundational ideology by which Roberts related to God and to others. When a wrong (real or imagined) was suffered, payback was the only option. And since Roberts could not exact his revenge directly upon God and make God *pay*, he would instead make other innocent young girls *pay* for the death of his infant daughter. Because, as the pervasive ideology goes, *someone has to pay*. According to the survivors, Roberts said,

"I'm angry at God and I need to punish some Christian girls to get even with Him."[5]

In an increasingly litigious America, often the first thought people have upon suffering a wrong is *someone has to pay*. The option of absorbing the blow and ending the cycle of payback goes unexplored. The very notion of nonresponse is viewed as foolish and even *wrong*. The liturgy of a payback culture is simple: someone has to pay. But the ideology of payback always leads to an escalation of sin and the ultimate triumph of evil. In his suicide note Roberts wrote, "I'm filled with so much hate towards myself, towards God, and an unimaginable emptiness."[6]

Hate. Revenge. Punishment. Payback. Getting even. These destructive concepts had become a black hole from which Charles Roberts could not escape. For nine years these ideas had festered, and once Roberts crossed the event horizon into the black hole of exponential hatred, the end was inevitable— it would end only in violence and death. Once we begin to play the game of payback and getting even, we enter a dangerous realm that can lead to unimagined consequences. Revenge and retaliation are the seeds of demonic ideas. Payback is the impetus for our most destructive actions. The lust for revenge has left entire nations in ruins. Hitler was driven by the need to make someone pay. Whether it was for the German humiliation in the Treaty of Versailles or his personal humiliation as a failed art student, someone had to pay. Those who are driven by revenge and payback are like a tornado lost in a self-absorbed vortex, bringing destruction wherever they go.

Charles Roberts's soul had become a tornado of destruction, and on a sunny fall morning he entered a small, one-room Amish schoolhouse armed with a .9mm handgun, a 12-gauge shotgun, a .30-06 rifle, two knives, and six hundred rounds of ammunition. Driven by hate, Roberts had ceased to be human and had now become a monster desperately trying to erase the image of God from his soul. In the schoolhouse there were twenty-six students and a teacher. Earlier that morning the class had prayed the Lord's Prayer. Children's voices praying: "Forgive us our trespasses as we forgive those who trespass against us...deliver us from evil." Entering the schoolhouse, Roberts ordered the children to lie facedown at the front of the room near the blackboard. The teacher and the boys were allowed to leave. He kept the ten girls—ten girls, ages six to thirteen. Roberts then barricaded the doors, bound the girls with duct tape, and announced, "I'm going to make you pay for my daughter." At 11:05 a.m., three shotgun blasts were followed by rapid-fire pistol shots. Charles Roberts had shot all ten girls in the head. Five died, five survived. Roberts completed his descent into the abyss by turning the gun on himself. Meanwhile, Roberts's wife, Amy, was at a Moms In Touch prayer group at a local Presbyterian church.

Unspeakable evil had invaded tranquility and brought life-shattering tragedy to the Amish community of Nickel Mines, Pennsylvania. It came in the most hideous form of all—child sacrifice, the slaughter of the innocents. Ten little girls shot in the head. Five dead; five in critical condition. It doesn't get any worse than that. And this could have been the end of the story. It could have been only the horror story of a madman and his senseless massacre. But this was not the end of the story. As the world shuddered from news of the Nickel Mines tragedy, the world would soon be stunned by a demonstration of radical forgiveness—forgiveness that transcended tragedy.

Within hours of the killings, a group of men from the Amish community went to Amy Roberts's house to express...*forgiveness!* They brought gifts of food to Amy and her children, telling Amy they had forgiven her husband and held no animosity toward her. They also promised to help her in the future by providing for her what she might need. Later that evening an Amish man visited Charles Roberts's father to offer his comfort. "He stood there for an hour, and he held that man in his arms and said, 'We forgive you.'"[7] In the days following, Roberts's parents received many more visits from members of the Amish community offering condolences and expressing forgiveness.

On the evening of the killings, as a grieving Amish family gathered in their home around the coffin of a little girl murdered in the schoolhouse shooting, the slain girl's grandfather told the younger children, "We shouldn't think evil of the man who did this." The same man later told the Associated Press, "I hope they [Roberts's widow and children] stay around here. They'll have lots of friends and a lot of support."[8]

Five days later when the Roberts family gathered to bury the gunman in the cemetery of Georgetown United Methodist Church, more than half of the seventy-five mourners were from the Amish community. Some of the Amish mourners who gathered around Amy Roberts and offered her hugs of support were parents who just days earlier had buried their own children. A Roberts family member described it this way.

> About thirty-five or forty Amish came to the burial. They shook our hands and cried. They embraced Amy and the children. There were no grudges, no hard feelings, only forgiveness. It's just hard to believe that they were able to do that.[9]

Only forgiveness. The Amish had only one way to respond to the most wicked of all transgressions: only forgiveness. There was no talk of reprisal, revenge, getting even, or making someone pay. Only forgiveness. They imitated Christ by offering only forgiveness. They took up the cross by responding with only forgiveness. They lived the Sermon on the Mount by demonstrating only forgiveness. They understood there was only one way to bring about healing—only forgiveness. When people from around the nation, moved by the tragedy, sent money to assist the Amish families who had lost children, the Amish families shared this money with the Roberts family. What can explain this kind of generosity? Only forgiveness.

> Radical forgiveness is what it means to take up the cross and follow Jesus.

The funeral director who witnessed the actions of the Amish community at Roberts's burial recalled the moving moment in these words.

> I was lucky enough to be at the cemetery when the Amish families of the children who had been killed came to greet Amy Roberts and offer their forgiveness. And that is something I'll never forget, not ever. I knew that I was witnessing a miracle.[10]

The Amish act of forgiveness changed the story line coming out of Nickel Mines. Instead of the Nickel Mines *tragedy*, media outlets began to speak of the Nickel Mines *miracle*. Forgiveness changed the story line from the horror of murder to the miracle of forgiveness. The miracle of Nickel Mines is a deliberate echo of the miracle of the cross. How is it that we don't speak of the cross of Christ as a tragedy, which was, after all, the murder of an innocent man? It's because on Good Friday Jesus changed the story line when he chose to absorb the blow and respond only with forgiveness. This change in the story line of Good Friday is what the Father endorsed on Easter Sunday in the resurrection.

The Amish of Nickel Mines understood that they were not just recipients of the forgiveness that flows from the cross—but that they were to be active practitioners of the same kind of costly forgiveness. And at its heart, radical forgiveness is what it means to take up the cross and follow Jesus. Jesus carried his cross to Golgotha, and there upon that cross extended forgiveness to his murderers. This is the radical act of cross carrying and enemy forgiving, which Jesus calls us to follow. And as hard as it was for Jesus to pray from the cross, "Father, forgive them"—it was no less hard for the Nickel Mines parents to offer forgiveness to the Roberts family. But as some of the Amish elders said, "We have to forgive. Refusing to forgive is not an option. It's just a normal part of our living. It's just standard Christian forgiveness."[11]

Just standard Christian forgiveness? Some might beg to differ. That the Amish act of forgiveness in the Nickel Mines murders was international news may say something about how *substandard* post-Constantine Christianity has become. But whether we regard it as standard or exceptional, this is the Jesus kind of radical forgiveness that captures the imagination of a world hell-bent on revenge. In the aftermath of the murders and the miracle of forgiveness, news commentators wondered if the Amish of Nickel Mines had perhaps initially met to formalize their decision to forgive. The book *Amish Grace* addresses this question.

> How did the Amish decide so quickly to extend forgiveness? That question brought laughter from some Amish people we interviewed. "You mean some people actually thought we got together to plan forgiveness?" chuckled Katie, a seventy-five-year-old grandmother, as she worked in her kitchen. "Forgiveness was a decided issue," explained Bishop Eli. "It's just what we do as nonresistant people. It was spontaneous. It

was automatic. It was not a new kind of thing." Every Amish person we spoke with agreed: forgiveness for Roberts and grace for his family had begun as spontaneous expressions of faith, not as mandates from the church.[12]

The Amish as a nonviolent, nonretaliatory community have developed a culture where Christlike forgiveness is understood as the only option for a Christ follower. As such, they don't have to consider each case and weigh the merits of forgiveness versus retaliation. Forgiveness is simply understood as nonnegotiable for a Christian. That does not mean that forgiveness is necessarily easy. And it certainly doesn't mean that Christian victims of injustice somehow *don't mind*. As N. T. Wright observes, "Forgiveness does not mean 'I didn't mind' or 'it didn't matter.' I did mind and it did matter; otherwise there wouldn't be anything to forgive at all."[13]

On that tragic day in October of 2006, blood was shed in an Amish schoolhouse. Ever since Cain killed Abel, the way of the world has been for shed blood to cry out for more shed blood. The human appetite for the shedding of blood seems to be insatiable. The human race has left a bloody bequest—a history written in blood and a map whose borders are drawn in blood. But the writer of Hebrews tells us that in coming to Christ, we have come to "the sprinkled blood that speaks a better word than the blood of Abel."*

A Blood Cry for Forgiveness

The blood of Abel cried out for revenge and brought a curse upon Cain. But the blood of Jesus cries out for forgiveness and brings a blessing upon the sinner. Those who believe in the forgiving blood of Jesus have abandoned the need for

---

* Hebrews 12:24

bloody revenge. Thus Michael Hardin writes, "For the Amish, the blood of their little girls did not cry out for retaliation, for vengeance. Rather, the blood of the Amish girls cried out in the heart of the Amish community, 'Forgiveness.'"[14]

Yes, I believe the blood of those little girls has a voice—a voice that whispers *forgive*. Had not those girls prayed a short while earlier, "Forgive us our trespasses, as we forgive those who trespass against us" and "deliver us from evil"? Who knew that the trespass they would need to forgive would be their own murder? And what about the prayer to be delivered from evil? Did that prayer go unanswered? I don't believe so. Though they were not delivered from the evil of murder, they were delivered from the evil of being *defined* by evil. Those little Amish girls are not remembered merely as victims but as martyrs for the gospel of forgiveness. Evil was not allowed to write the last word on their lives. Because of the community they belonged to, forgiveness had the last word, and they were delivered from evil.

The act of forgiveness at Nickel Mines did not erase the tragedy, but it did transcend it. Transcending evil is not the same thing as ignoring evil. Christian forgiveness in the face of real evil is not a liberal fantasy of pretending that evil isn't all that bad; Christian forgiveness is a means of transcending evil and refusing to engage with evil on its own terms. Because the Amish of Nickel Mines chose to forgive, evil did not have the last word. When Charles Roberts fired his guns, he hoped to write the final sentence—a sentence of revenge written in blood. But with the simple (or not so simple) act of forgiveness, the story line was changed. Charles Roberts did not have the last word. The last word was not about payback. The Amish were able to rescript the tragedy—a tragedy they had made no choice to participate in. And although they had no choice about participating in the tragedy, they did have a choice as to what role they would play and how the story would end. Through forgiveness they would not play the role of eternal victim. Instead, they would play the redemptive role of Christ follower. They would choose to absorb the blow, end the cycle of revenge, and recast the story in different terms. Instead of a cast comprised only of villain and victims, now the story would add saints and healers to the cast.

If the Nickel Mines story were to be made into a movie, it would not be a horror film or even a tragedy (though tragedy plays an enormous role in the story). Instead, a movie on the Nickel Mines shootings would somehow end up being a film about hope and healing. The tears that would be shed in the theater would not be just tears of grief; they would also be the tears of joy as the human soul responds to the poignant beauty of forgiveness. This is the power of forgiveness—a power to transcend tragedy and turn heartbreak into hope. This is something *only* forgiveness can do. The only way the tragedy of Good Friday can end in the hope of Easter Sunday is for the victim to be recast as saint as he absorbs the blow and prays, "Father, forgive them."

In the next chapter we will explore the complex interaction between forgiveness and justice, but at this point I want to say something about the Amish (and I believe Christian) reluctance to engage in punitive justice (justice motivated solely by a desire to punish). Though there is a place in Christian justice for protection, restitution, and restoration, the desire for punishment for punishment's sake must, at best, be regarded as highly suspect. Too often the only purpose punitive justice serves is to satisfy our lust for vengeance, and the spirit of vengeance has no place in the Christian community.

During the first four centuries of the church, punitive justice was not part of the Christian concept of justice. Yet sadly, through the centuries the biblical concept of restorative justice has been distorted into a justice that is largely punitive and vindictive. Consider how foreign the words of Augustine sound in our ears, who, fearing a death sentence would be issued upon the murderers of some of his friends, wrote in 412 to Judge Marcellinus:

> We do not wish the suffering of the servants of God avenged by the affliction of precisely similar injuries in the way of retaliation....Be not provoked by the atrocity of their sinful deeds to gratify the passion of revenge, but rather be moved by the wounds which these deeds have inflicted on their own souls to exercise a desire to heal them.[15]

Augustine's concept of justice was that it must be motivated by a desire to heal the souls of those who had committed murder, and not merely to satisfy a lust for revenge. Indeed, this sounds foreign in the ears of a culture nurtured in vengeance. Keep in mind that as the architect of the Just War theory, Augustine was no ultraliberal in the modern sense of the word. Nevertheless, a justice that was purely punitive and did nothing more than satisfy the carnal desire for vengeance was abhorrent and thoroughly un-Christian to Augustine. His position on the matter was neither extreme nor unique; it was simply the accepted view of the early church. But things have changed dramatically in the post-Constantine era of the church and raises the troubling question: *Whom would Jesus execute?*

For the Amish of Nickel Mines, revenge (even if the gunman had survived) was out of the question. Acting as followers of Christ, they chose to forgive the murderer and show mercy to his family. They also chose to tear down the schoolhouse that was the scene of such horrific evil. A half mile down the road they built a new schoolhouse. They named it New Hope. It could not be more aptly named. In the face of the most ghastly tragedy, only one thing could give the Amish of Nickel Mines new hope—and that was forgiveness. Again we are reminded that without forgiveness there is no future. But with forgiveness, the eclipse of goodness that marks Good Friday gives way to the dawn of hope that is Easter Sunday.

Christian forgiveness is neither ignorance nor amnesia. Forgiveness both knows and remembers. Forgiveness does not call us to forget. Who can forget Good Friday? Or Auschwitz? Or Nickel Mines? Christian forgiveness does not call us to forget but to exhaust evil by ending the cycle of revenge. Forgiveness is not pretending that evil didn't happen or trying to tell ourselves it wasn't really evil. This may be an acceptable approach within Buddhism, which denies the existence of evil, but this approach is unacceptable within Christianity. For the Christian whose faith is rooted in Good Friday, the existence of real evil—both human and demonic—is undeniable. Jesus *was* crucified, and it *was* unjust, and it *was* evil. But evil does not have the last word on Good Friday. (That's why it's called *Good* Friday and not *Black* Friday.) Through absorbing evil in forgiveness without vengeful retaliation, Jesus overcame evil. And his resurrection on Easter Sunday was not the rise of vengeance but the triumph of forgiveness.

This is why the apostle Paul, writing to first-century Christians living in a very unjust world, could say: "Repay no one evil for evil" and "Do not be overcome by evil, but overcome evil with good."* When Jesus prayed from the cross, "Father, forgive them," he overcame evil with good. There was nothing more evil could do. Evil had run its course and exhausted itself upon Jesus. When Jesus's only response was to offer forgiveness, evil had quite simply been overcome by good. Evil had reached the end of the line. Evil had done its worst and run out of steam.

---

* Romans 12:17, 21

The Triumph of the Cross

In his letter to the Colossians, Paul says that, at the cross, "having disarmed the powers and authorities, he [Jesus] made a public spectacle of them, triumphing over them by the cross."* How does the cross triumph over the principalities and powers—the power structures (both human and demonic) that have kept humanity engaged in the endless cycle of revenge and payback? By absorbing the blow and offering forgiveness to those committing the crime of deicide—the murder of God. This is why the final word from the cross is, "It is finished."† The endless cycle of revenge and paybacks was finished at the cross! Now forgiveness would take the stage and begin to remake a world according to the goodness of forgiveness.

> *Without forgiveness there is no future. But with forgiveness, the eclipse of goodness that marks Good Friday gives way to the dawn of hope that is Easter Sunday.*

Forgiveness changes everything. The goodness of Good Friday is the goodness of forgiveness. Though still a tragic story, the story that emerges from Nickel Mines is ultimately a good story. This is what forgiveness can do. When you choose to forgive, you go from victim to saint in your own story. When you choose to forgive, it becomes *your* story, not the offender's story. When you choose to forgive, you are given the potential to transcend tragedy. When you choose to forgive, though

---

* Colossians 2:15, NIV
† John 19:30

you are touched by evil, you are not defined by it. When you choose to forgive, you overcome evil with good. In the end, your story will not be a bad story but a good story. If you can believe in Good Friday and Easter Sunday, you can believe that your encounter with evil can ultimately become a good story—a story where evil is overcome by good.

As those who believe in the victory of the cross, we need to reclaim the triumph of forgiveness in the realm of imagination. We live in a culture that constantly celebrates and glorifies vengeful and vigilante violence—especially in the realm of entertainment. This is partly because it is only through a perverted concept of justice that our culture can *justify* its obsession with the pornography of violence, from movies to video games. In the competitive and lucrative video game market, the quest has become to see who can produce the most realistic and graphic depictions of violence and bloodletting. What was outrageously violent ten years ago is now considered tame.

But to justify this escalation in violence, the concept of justice must first be debased into vengeance. Thus the imaginations of young boys are being captured and shaped by a destructive obsession with revenge and payback. Manhood is defined by the ability to exact your revenge through violence. By this definition, Jesus was not a "real" man. And if you don't recognize the lie of Satan in that, you're not paying attention. Pastors and Christian leaders need to insist that the pornography of violence is at least as un-Christian as sexual pornography, and ultimately not all that different, as both are attempts to dehumanize others and relegate people to the status of objects to be used or abused for our own satisfaction.

A rejection of this antihuman view is the reason why it was Christians who brought an end to the gladiatorial games of ancient Rome. In Christ they believed that violent bloodshed was finished at the cross and that in the new world that God is in the process of creating in Christ, violence as punitive justice or perverse entertainment has no place. The early Christians believed that violence as entertainment is a sinful affront to human dignity. When Christians look at the violence inflicted upon Christ at the cross, it should make them cry out, "Never again." Never again will we endorse the use of violence upon our fellow creatures who bear the image of God. The cross of Christ needs to be the place where all of that is finished. The cross of Christ needs to be (and is!) the beginning point of God's new world.

> *The cross liberates the imagination to discover how forgiveness transcends tragedy and how good triumphs over evil.*

In Christ it is forgiveness that is glorified, not violence, and not vengeance. The cross liberates the imagination to discover how forgiveness transcends tragedy and how good triumphs over evil. When we choose to forgive, we rewrite the story line. When we forgive, we are enabled to recast ourselves in our own story. When we forgive, we reclaim the story for ourselves—no longer is it a tragic story whose script we must follow that is being forced upon us.

With forgiveness, the story takes a dramatic turn toward an alternate ending—an alternate ending that corresponds with Easter Sunday. Without forgiveness, evil is allowed to write the final word—and often that word is *retaliation*. In this way evil is passed on from generation to generation as a demonic virus, and generations of human lives are ruined while the virus of evil lives on. But forgiveness changes all that. When the virus of recalcitrant evil encounters the forgiveness of the cross, it is finally overcome. This is the kind of radical forgiveness taught and modeled by Jesus Christ—a forgiveness that empowers human beings to change the story and transcend tragedy.

6

FORGIVENESS AND JUSTICE

N COMING TO terms with the call of Christ for his disciples to be practitioners of radical forgiveness, we inevitably run into the thorny question of how forgiveness relates to justice. The psalmist envisions a meeting of mercy and truth, an embrace between justice and peace.

> Mercy and Truth meet;
> Justice and Peace kiss.
> —PSALM 85:10, AUTHOR'S TRANSLATION

But in what way? How can mercy and truth meet? How can justice and peace kiss? Is there a way in which the mercy of forgiveness can kiss the truth of justice and it not be a Judas kiss of betrayal? In forgiving, are we just kissing justice good-bye? If we forgive the offender for his or her transgression and let that person *just get away with it*, hasn't justice been betrayed? So we are faced with the troubling question of whether forgiveness and justice are at loggerheads. Do we have to choose one or the other—justice or forgiveness? Are there times when forgiveness and justice are mutually exclusive?

113

We need to be honest enough to admit that at times forgiveness and justice can appear irreconcilable. The philosopher Nietzsche went so far as to suggest that forgiving extreme unjust actions are part of what he called *slave morality*—the morality of the weak. Operating from a foundation that denies the existence of God, Nietzsche saw it like this: the strong have the capacity to gain revenge, but forgiveness is the only recourse available to the weak. According to Nietzsche, forgiveness is a means by which the weak manipulate the strong. Thus a morality that insists upon forgiveness in all situations is, in reality, an expression of weakness.

Of course the Christian will have to ask himself this question: When Jesus said, "Father, forgive them," was that an act of strength or an act of weakness? In the drama of Good Friday, who is the one who exhibits strength? Is it Caiaphas? Is it Pilate? Is it Jesus? Caiaphas and Pilate represented the undeniable strength of the Roman Empire and the religious system that colluded with it. They possessed the power to sentence men to death—from one perspective the greatest power of all. But what strength and what power are present when an innocent man undergoing a state-sponsored execution forgives his executioners? Is this merely a morality of weakness? Nietzsche's slave morality? No doubt the Christian has a ready-made answer, but still the perplexing questions pertaining to the complicated relationship between forgiveness and justice remain.

Understanding Justice

Part of the problem is the very concept of justice. What do we mean by justice? Justice is a word everyone thinks they understand, but the moment we go to define it, things get tricky. The Merriam-Webster dictionary defines *justice* as: "the maintenance or administration of what is just especially by the impartial adjustment of conflicting claims or the assignment of merited rewards or punishments." In all honesty, that probably doesn't help us very much—it may be something of a tacit admission that for all our use of the word *justice*, we're still not quite sure what it is. In the context of our own experience with what we deem to be unfair treatment, the use of the word *justice* probably has something to do with protection or punishment or recompense, or some combination of the three. So when we see ourselves as a victim seeking justice, we generally mean we are seeking *protection* from those who are harming us or would harm us; or we are seeking the *punishment* of those who have harmed us; or we are seeking *recompense* for what we have lost through the unjust actions of others. Of course this is what our legal and criminal justice systems attempt to deliver. But things are never quite as simple as that.

For one thing, justice is often a matter of perspective. Being sincerely convinced of the rightness of our own cause is no guarantee that we are actually in the right. Deception concerning the rightness of our cause may be the most common form of self-deception. The very concept of justice would tell us that in every war at least one side is unjust. But who ever goes to war not believing that their cause is just? If you have ever been involved in helping mediate disputes, you know how complicated things can be. Solomon wisely, if perhaps wearily, observed, "The first to present his case seems right, till another comes forward and questions him."* Bob Dylan says it this way:

> It's a restless hungry feeling
> That don't mean no one no good,
> When ev'rything I'm a-sayin'
> You can say it just as good.
> You're right from your side,

---

* Proverbs 18:17, NIV

I'm right from mine.
We're both just one too many mornings
An' a thousand miles behind.[1]

"You're right from your side, I'm right from mine." Isn't this the way it often is? Justice is not always black and white. Sometimes it's barely discernable. Who is right and who is wrong can be enormously complicated. And when we are involved in a dispute, it would serve us well to remember that our perspective may be limited. Miroslav Volf astutely reminds us, "When we are looking at each other through the sights of our guns we see only the rightness of our own cause. We think more about how to enlarge our power than to enlarge our thinking."[2] Trying to win an argument (much less a war!) isn't usually a very good way of arriving at the truth. Truth is too often sacrificed for the sake of the argument. When we have a stake in the matter, we have a natural tendency to oversimplify what constitutes justice, and often *justice* is little more than *me getting my way.*

Imagine you are involved in a property dispute with your neighbor. The neighbor has constructed a toolshed that extends three feet onto your property. You don't want a toolshed occupying three feet of your property. Attempts to rectify the impasse with your neighbor fail, so you take the matter to court. The judge hears the case, decides on your behalf, and orders the toolshed removed. You are satisfied. But has justice been done? Perhaps. Certainly you may think so. But whose justice? At what point in the past do we start keeping score in order to determine what is just? What if the judge issued an alternative verdict: "I have heard your case, considered your arguments, and I have decided to return both of your properties to the Native Americans from whom it was stolen a hundred and fifty years ago." Is this perhaps justice? One might argue it's a different *kind* of justice. It might seem just in one perspective but patently unjust in another. When we talk about justice, we often do so within artificial boundaries. We mean justice in a contemporary context, not a historic context. We mean limited justice, not overall justice; we mean justice for me, not for everyone. We should be suspicious of those who are too zealous and too confident about achieving justice in an absolute sense. The truth is, we probably *don't* want justice as much as we claim. As Miroslav Volf observes, "If you want justice and nothing but justice, you will inevitably get injustice."[3]

But this is not acquiescence to anarchy. The need for the protection of justice is unquestionable. Society has an obligation to protect the weak from the strong and to guard the citizen from the criminal. Thus the apostle Paul can speak of those engaged in civil law enforcement as, "God's servant for your good."[*] Likewise, we have courts with the authority to order restitution with the intention of righting past wrongs.

The matter of punitive justice (punishment) is more complex, but few would doubt that punitive justice has a certain role in a civil society. When the system works, it actually helps assist the victim to engage in forgiveness. In criminal cases the state bears the burden of justice, while the victim is free to forgive, if they choose. In criminal cases the victim's forgiveness has little bearing on the state's exercise of justice. So that if a rape victim chooses to follow the call of Christ to practice radical forgiveness, the state will view that as all good and well, but will still mete out punishment. This is the ideal. This is government at its best. This is the authority that God has delegated to civil government.[†]

Again I stress, forgiveness does not necessarily call us to forget—forgiveness calls us to end the cycle of revenge. Part

---

[*]   Romans 13:4

[†]   See Romans 13:1ff.

of the reason we can dare to end the cycle of revenge is that we have left the matter of justice to God. We forgive, and we leave justice to God. In certain situations that means leaving the matter of justice to the state, which possesses the sword and can act to a limited extent as a representative of divine justice.

Justice and Faith

Ultimately our hope for justice lies with our faith in God, not government. Governments can be tyrannical; judges can be bribed; police can be corrupt. From a human perspective, justice is not always accomplished—even when all involved are honest and well meaning. For an atheist like Nietzsche, forgiveness of egregious injustice may indeed be weakness. But for those who believe in a God who is personally committed to the cause of justice, forgiveness is an act of faith, not weakness. The choice to forgive is not an exoneration of the criminal; it is a choice to end the cycle of revenge and leave the matter of justice in the hands of God.

This perspective on justice helps us understand what is known as the *imprecatory psalms*—the *cursing* psalms. These are the angry psalms that plead for God to do justice by inflicting his wrath upon the wicked. What we learn from the imprecatory psalms is that rage against injustice belongs before God. Instead of holding rage against injustice in our heart where it is allowed to fester and corrupt, we place our rage before the throne of God, recognizing that God and God alone is capable of judging the world in righteousness. Anger against deep injustice is unavoidable. That anger can be brought before God in an appropriate way through the imprecatory psalms. In the midst of our unjust world, we cry out to God for him to judge the world and establish justice, and at times we do so with great passion. But that is where such passion belongs—before the throne of God and not festering in our heart or heaped upon our enemy's head. Dietrich Bonhoeffer deals directly and insightfully with the sometimes troubling imprecatory psalms in his book *Life Together*, a book he wrote while leading an underground seminary in Nazi Germany.

> Can we, then, pray the imprecatory psalms?...A psalm that we cannot utter as prayer, that makes us falter and horrifies us, is a hint to us that here Someone else is praying, not we; that the One who...is invoking God's judgment...is none other than Jesus Christ himself. He it is who is praying here, and not only here but in the whole Psalter...through the mouth of his Church.[4]

The purpose of the "furious parts of the Psalms," as C. S. Lewis called them, has to do with placing our anger concerning violent injustice before God and trusting God to bring about justice. But a word of caution: The imprecatory psalms are how the saints have prayed concerning violent and murderous injustice—from ancient Semitic warlords to Nazis. But it is *not* how we are to pray concerning our brothers and sisters in Christ with whom we simply cannot get along. How Dietrich Bonhoeffer might pray concerning Hitler is not how we are to pray concerning irritating church members. The prayer of imprecatory rage is a response to the monstrous, not the petty.

Justitia (Lady Justice), the Roman goddess of justice, has long helped form the Western concept of justice. She is depicted as holding scales in her left hand, a sword in her right hand, and wearing a blindfold. The scales are the scales of justice, the sword is the sword of judgment, and the blindfold represents impartiality. To this day the Roman goddess Justitia is the iconic image of justice in the Western world, frequently adorning courthouses. But there are problems with this depiction of justice. For one thing, do we really want someone who is blind-folded wielding a sword?

I'm going to suggest that blind, or even impartial justice, is *not* necessarily what we find when dealing with the God of the Bible. Instead, with his eyes wide open, God seems to have a predisposition to show a certain kind of partiality to the poor, the widow, the orphan, and the alien. The entire prophetic tradition of the Hebrew prophets bears witness to this. The most common way the word *justice* is used in the Old Testament prophetic books has to do with upholding the cause of those who are in danger of forming a permanent underclass in society. Though it may offend our modern democratic penchant for radical egalitarianism, the witness of Scripture is clear that God is committed to upholding the cause of the weak and the poor in a way that he is not committed to upholding the cause of the strong and rich.

Furthermore, God's concept of justice as revealed in Scripture seems to have much more to do with covenant and relationship than with cold, hard, impartial justice. God's highest commitment seems to be to covenant and reconciliation—a commitment that, at times, seems to eclipse what we might call justice. This is especially true when we consider God's covenantal interaction with Israel in the Old Testament.

In the fourth chapter of the Book of Judges, we are told: "The people of Israel again did what was evil in the sight of the LORD."* This is a recurrent theme in the Book of Judges. As a result of their evil, God subjected Israel to the Canaanites. But when Israel cried to the Lord, he heard and delivered them. (Another recurrent theme!) But then in the fifth chapter, this is called justice.† It seems as though justice is what happens when God acts on behalf of his covenant people,

---

* Judges 4:1
† Judges 5:11

regardless of the rightness of their cause. At this point in the historical narrative of Scripture, God seems more interested in achieving a faithful relationship with Israel than in achieving impartial justice between the warring clans of the ancient Near East.

To say it another way, God interprets justice in terms of relationship and reconciliation, not necessarily in terms of what we might consider fair. And since God's ultimate goal seems to be reconciliation and not merely retribution or even the redressing of wrongs, this is why forgiveness cannot run its full course and achieve the ultimate goal of reconciliation unless the offending party engages in genuine repentance—a repentance where sin is acknowledged, named as sin, and forsaken. But repentance must be correctly understood. Repentance is not the punitive practice of penance but the transforming practice of facing the truth and turning away from sin. This alone makes final reconciliation possible.

Therefore, if we are sinned against by a person who in some way harms us, we can forgive them in the sense of making a decision to end the cycle of revenge and leave the matter of justice with God. But for there to be the possibility of reconciliation and the restoration of relationship, there must be repentance. The restoration of relationship without repentance is a *cheap reconciliation*, which is not endorsed in Scripture. This indeed would be a *slave morality*, and it is not what the Bible calls us to. But we must be careful not to confuse repentance and retribution. When the offending party can sincerely say, "I am sorry," the door has been opened for reconciliation. And we who forgive as followers of Christ must be willing to walk through that door and leave the matter of punitive justice in the hands of God (which in some situations may mean the state). Let me say it as simply as I can: the goal of forgiveness *and the goal of justice* is reconciliation, not retribution.

The Goal—Reconciliation

In its most basic form, forgiveness is the choice to resist responding to evil with evil, to resist responding to hate with hate, to resist responding to violence with violence, to resist responding to malice with malice. This is the basic requirement of forgiveness. But that alone does not achieve the final goal of justice, which is reconciliation. For reconciliation to occur, there must be repentance on the part of the offender. Forgiveness can happen unilaterally, but reconciliation requires the participation of both parties. This is what the apostle Paul sets forth in Romans 12:17–21:

> Repay no one evil for evil, but give thought to do what is honorable in the sight of all. If possible, so far as it depends on you, live peaceably with all. Beloved, never avenge yourselves, but leave it to the wrath of God, for it is written, "Vengeance is mine, I will repay, says the Lord." To the contrary, "if your enemy is hungry, feed him; if he is thirsty, give him something to drink; for by so doing you will heap burning coals on his head." Do not be overcome by evil, but overcome evil with good.

A number of years ago a church member came to me with a complaint against another member of the church. (Pastors just love it when this happens.) His complaint involved a disputed $500 deposit on a rental property that he owned. His side of the story was complicated, and though I could see his point, I wasn't entirely sure he was right. But to tell the truth, I wasn't all that interested in who was right. I'm not a judge; I'm a pastor. And as a pastor, I wasn't nearly as interested in justice as I was in reconciliation. I wanted these two church members to be friends and get along. I decided it was worth $500 to me. So I told the offended church member this. "What

I want you to do is to forgive. I want you to forgive your sister in Christ and let the matter go. I will personally give you the $500. I'll pay what you are owed at my own expense. You won't be out any money. For my sake, I ask you to forgive your sister." The result was that he got mad at me and left the church. He wasn't interested in reconciliation. He wasn't even interested in justice. What he wanted was retribution, pure and simple. He wanted to stick it to someone he didn't like and see that person squirm. He wanted her to be humiliated. He wanted to use me as an authority figure to lower the boom on his enemy. When I instead pleaded for reconciliation, even to the point of being willing to cover the offense at my own expense... I got *crucified*. That experience helped me understand God's perspective on justice.

> *Repentance is not the punitive practice of penance but the transforming practice of facing the truth and turning away from sin.*

For God, the goal of justice is always reconciliation. Punitive justice may at times be part of the necessary journey there, but reconciliation is always the goal. Thus God's greatest act of justice is to save the sinner—and God does so by the "injustice" of grace. If we are ever going to understand and get along with the God revealed in the Bible, we are going to have to come to terms with the "injustice" of his grace. This is precisely what the elder brother in the parable of the prodigal son was unwilling to do.

Of course, the parable of the prodigal son was Jesus's response to the Pharisees when they criticized his practice of welcoming and sharing meals with sinners. In the parable the elder brother was unwilling to accept that the father's highest commitment was to relationship and not rules. For the elder brother it was unacceptable for a rule breaker to be received back into relationship simply on the basis of repentance and grace. But for the father it was unacceptable that his returning son would *not* be accepted back into relationship. This was the impasse between the father and the elder son.*

This was also the impasse between Jesus and the Pharisees. It involves the complicated issue of how forgiveness and justice go together. And though it is complicated, it seems to come down to this: For the Pharisees, rules were more important than relationship, and retribution was more important than reconciliation. For Jesus, relationship was more important than rules, and reconciliation was more important than retribution. For the Pharisees, the rule of law had to be satisfied. For Jesus, the broken relationship had to be restored. It was precisely at this point that Jesus and the Pharisees disagreed concerning what constituted justice. For the Pharisees, the stoning of a sinner was justice. For Jesus, sitting at a table with reconciled sinners was justice. Pharisees will always see God's relational priority paradigm as injustice. But the relational priority paradigm is the very thing that God calls justice.

So we're back to the question of whose justice we are talking about when we speak of justice. The sight of the younger son wearing the father's robe, ring, and shoes and dancing at a reconciliation party was injustice in the eyes of the elder brother. But having the estranged son back at home was the only thing the father would accept as justice. The squandered inheritance was gone. It was lost. It could not be recovered. What *could* be recovered was the broken relationship. This is what would constitute justice. So it was, and so it is. The past cannot be fully undone. Every past wrong cannot be made right. What can

---

* See Luke 15.

happen is reconciliation. Not *cheap reconciliation*, but the costly reconciliation based in repentance and grace. This is what God calls justice.

If our goal is to achieve perfect fairness through cold, hard, blind justice, indeed some problems may well be intractable and perhaps impossible to solve. Will peace in the Israeli-Palestinian conflict be achieved through classical justice alone? I don't see how. To undo all the wrongs that have been done through the pursuit of classical justice alone seems to be utterly impossible—a fool's errand. The justice that *can* come about in the Israeli-Palestinian conflict is the justice that understands the final goal as reconciliation. So when I worked with an Israeli and a Palestinian who are cooperating to provide toys for poor children in Gaza, I see the kind of justice that has the potential to bring about peace.

As Christians, we must reject the temptation to take sides in these intractable conflicts, often at the cost of delegitimizing and even dehumanizing the other side. When we take sides, we become a pawn in someone's game and offer nothing more than cheap, politicized "solutions." We remain part of the problem when we reduce justice to justice for one side. (And it is all the worse when we arrive at our conclusions through misreading our Bibles!) That's when we fall into the madness of thinking peace and justice can be achieved through bombs and missiles.

In the Israeli-Palestinian conflict, Christians are not called to take Israel's side; Christians are called to imitate Israel's Messiah—the Messiah who prioritized reconciliation, taught enemy-love, and gave the world the radical idea of forgiving seventy times seven. The way of Jesus is the alternative way, where justice does not come by suicide bombs or predator drones. This is the way we are called to bear witness to. This alone is the justice that can heal the world. This is justice that Amos longed to roll like a mighty river.* This is not justice that is blind and holding a sword; this is justice that looks on with love and offers a healing hand. As Reinhold Niebuhr has said, "Anything short of love cannot be perfect justice."[5]

If your concept of justice is to make sure that everyone gets "what they deserve," you are going to have a hard time getting along with Jesus. This is the very kind of justice that Jesus stands against and came to save us from. A world bent on the justice of giving people "what they deserve" is a world that is endlessly cruel and marked by alienation, violence, and war. The concept of retributive justice is what fuels the endless escalation of violence in the worst places of our world—from troubled inner cities to the troubled Middle East. Retributive justice has the horrible tendency to degenerate into *my justice*. And *my justice* is inevitably someone else's injustice. This is not the justice that saves—this is the justice that kills.

Justice Reinterpreted by Mercy Is Redefined as Reconciliation

The cross of Christ is not the triumph of justice—Calvary was the scene of the ultimate injustice! The cross of Christ is the triumph of forgiveness. The cross is where ultimate injustice encounters ultimate forgiveness in the words, "Father, forgive them." The cross is where we do *not* get what we deserve. The cross is where judgment is passed over in favor of forgiveness so that the whole world might be reconciled. The cross is where justice is reinterpreted by mercy in order to be redefined as reconciliation. This alone is what God calls justice. This is where mercy and truth meet, where justice and peace kiss. The cross is the place where "mercy triumphs over

---

* Amos 5:24

126

judgment."* Good Friday was the day when mercy triumphed over judgment, because the Son of God abandoned his right to justice and instead asked the Father to forgive.

> *The cross is where justice is reinterpreted by mercy in order to be redefined as reconciliation. This alone is what God calls justice.*

In the movie *Gran Torino*, Clint Eastwood plays the character of Walt Kowalski, a racist, embittered, retired factory worker and Korean War veteran living in a deteriorating Detroit neighborhood dominated by Asian immigrants and gang violence. Walt has little relationship with his grown sons and their self-absorbed suburban families. His two loves are his dog, Daisy, and his cherished 1972 Ford Gran Torino. A family of Hmong immigrants from Southeast Asia live next door, and as part of a gang initiation, the teenage boy Thao is coerced into attempting to steal Walt's Gran Torino. Walt interrupts the attempted theft, and over time an improbable friendship develops between Walt and Thao. When the Hmong gang continues to harass Thao, Walt responds by beating one of the gang leaders and threatening further violence if they don't leave Thao alone. But the gang escalates the violence with a drive-by shooting of Thao's home and the brutal rape of Thao's sister. In the climactic scene of the film, Walt confronts the gang armed with only a cigarette lighter as he deliberately draws their gunfire and dies with his arms outstretched in the form of a cross.

Walt Kowalski had come to realize that violence would perpetuate itself in an endless cycle of revenge until someone

---

* James 2:13

absorbed the blow without retaliation. This is what Walt was willing to do. He would lay down his life for his friend—the *other* whom he had come to love. And whereas it is not a perfect parallel to Christ as he embraces the cross, it was a deliberate echo of Good Friday. And it's an amazing role for an actor who has built his career playing tough guys in pursuit of vigilante justice.

If God's goal of justice is reconciliation, and the cross is the place where God accomplishes his ultimate justice, then our concept of justice may need reworking. If Calvary is the place where mercy and truth meet, where justice and peace kiss, then we must liberate justice from the narrow and tired idea that justice is what happens when people "get what they deserve." If peace is to prevail and humanity be healed, we must do more than satisfy the law of retributive justice; we must find a way for reconciliation. This leads us straight into the mystery of redemption. The New Testament reveals what the Old Testament had only hinted at—that justice has more to do with finding a way to end the cycle of hostility and revenge than with giving each their due. It is the way of ending the hostility so that reconciliation can have a chance. Miroslav Volf touches on a key aspect of the mystery of redemption and God's triumph over evil when he observes:

> To triumph fully, evil needs two victories, not one. The first victory happens when an evil deed is perpetrated; the second victory, when evil is returned. After the first victory, evil would die if the second victory did not infuse it with new life.[6]

Justice as reconciliation is how the apostle Paul understands the cross when he says, "In Christ God was reconciling the world to himself, not counting their trespasses against them."*

Paul then goes on to say that the cross with all of its seeming injustice was in fact the triumph of the righteousness; in fact, Paul calls it the *justice* of God.† God's justice is not achieved by everyone getting what they deserve but by God choosing not to count our trespasses against us. The justice of reconciliation is what happened when God chose to answer the prayer his Son prayed from the cross: "Father, forgive them, for they know not what they do."

In answer to Jesus's prayer, there would be no retribution, no reprisal, no vengeful reckoning. Injustice had found a place to die—it died in Christ when he absorbed the blow on Good Friday without retaliation. And the resurrection of Christ was not only the Father's vindication of his Son; it was also the dawn of a new world founded on the justice of reconciliation and forgiveness. The first Easter Sunday saw justice and peace kiss so that the risen Son of God could say, "Peace be with you."‡ Ultimately, God's justice is found in God's mercy. This is how we are reconciled with God and with one another. This is how we are saved.

---

* 2 Corinthians 5:19
† 2 Corinthians 5:21
‡ John 20:19, 21

7

KILLING THE HOSTILITY

HOSTILITY. ENMITY. ACRIMONY. Animosity. Aggression. Malice. Malevolence. When these destructive vices are present in an individual, the problem is bad enough; but when they are present within groups, clans, tribes, parties, and nations, the consequences can be truly horrific. The human race has a tragic history of drawing lines in hostility and relating to the whole world as either the accepted us or the alienated them. World history is largely the story of how political borders came into being—and behind every border is a bloody story told in terms of us versus them. In a world of alienation, the us versus them scenario seems natural to us, as though it is the only way to understand the world. We seem to lack the imagination to envision life any other way.

But must it be this way? Must *us* versus *them* be our controlling paradigm? The New Testament challenges this. Specifically, the gospel of the cross calls us to rethink the *us* versus *them* paradigm—and for very good reason. The *us* versus *them* attitude of groupthink hostility is the source of humanity's most shameful crimes: racism, torture, war, and genocide. If the gospel is to offer solutions for mankind's greatest problems, and if the gospel is to have relevance beyond the realm of private piety and afterlife religion, it must be able to address the curse of deep-seated and historic hostility. The apostle Paul's theology of the cross is a gospel that addresses this very issue. Paul boldly states that the cross *kills* groupthink hostility. In the increasingly hostile world of the twenty-first century where the church is all too prone to participate in the *us* versus *them* mentality, this is a gospel we vitally need to recover.

Let's consider the human experience. Human beings are the most social of all of God's creatures. We cannot live any other way. We require a social existence not only for survival but also for definition. We understand ourselves in the context of the groups to which we belong. Who are we? We are our family, our religion, our nationality, our ethnicity, our class, our politics, and the football team we root for. "No man is an island, entire of itself."[1]

But who we *are* is often understood today most clearly in terms of who we *aren't*. We are *us* because we are not *them*. Unfortunately (at least, I consider this unfortunate!), the easiest way to unite people is to unite them *against* something. We are more prone to have passion for what we oppose than for what we support. Negativity is easily energized (especially on the Internet!). The tendency to define ourselves in the negative is most easily done if we can personify what we are not as a group of people—the dreaded *other*, the hated *them*. Skillful politicians understand this very well, and manipulative politicians know how to use it. Not to mention the devil.

And so we divide into our respective groups based on similar characteristics, shared opinion, and common interest. If we nurture the antagonism of groupthink hostility toward the *others*—the alienated *them*—that hostility can so corrupt our thinking that we deprive *them* of their full humanity. Once that is done, all things are permitted. To regard others as inhuman is to sanction actions that are inhumane. If the Nazi denies the humanity of the Jew, if the Serb denies the humanity of the Bosniak, if the Hutu denies the humanity of the Tutsi, then all things are permitted, including genocide. Of course, group-think hostility rarely results in the ultimate extreme of genocide, but the extreme serves to warn us just how dangerous cultivating hostility can be.

God's Peace Project

In the hostile world of hate, war, and genocide, a cross appears. The cross is God's peace project designed to end the hostility and achieve reconciliation. The cross not only achieves peace between God and the alienated sinner, but the cross is also the place where God forms a new humanity—a humanity saved from hostility. This is the theology of the cross that Paul sets forth in his letter to the Ephesians. And to show the effectiveness of the cross in "killing the hostility" and thereby achieving peace, Paul applies it to one of the most intractable *us* versus *them* divides of his day—the division between Jews and Gentiles.

> That he might create in himself one new humanity in place of the two, thus making peace, and might reconcile both groups to God in one body through the cross, thus putting to death that hostility ["thereby killing the hostility," esv].
>
> —Ephesians 2:15–16, nrsv

In his letter to the Ephesians, Paul is writing to the young, predominantly Gentile church of Ephesus on the west coast of Asia Minor (Turkey). These are people newly converted from the pagan religions of the Roman Empire to faith in Jesus Christ. He reminds these Gentile believers that in times past,

Gentiles were excluded and alienated from the commonwealth of Israel. Non-Jews were foreigners to the covenant, and as foreigners they were without hope of attaining full citizenship in the kingdom of God (the kingdom of God was understood as entirely synonymous with the nation of Israel). The Jewish mind of the first century understood citizenship in the kingdom of God (Israel) as based upon three crucial factors: ethnicity, circumcision, and Torah observance—all of which excluded Gentiles. The only way an ethnic Gentile could obtain the blessings and promises of Israel was to be circumcised and observe the cultural markers of the Torah—dietary laws, Sabbath observance, Jewish purification rites, and so forth. In other words, the only way a Gentile could become a citizen of Yahweh's kingdom was to become a Jew. So the Jewish thought was this: "To be accepted by God you must become one of us." But they should have known better.

> *If the gospel is to offer solutions for mankind's greatest problems, and if the gospel is to have relevance beyond the realm of private piety and afterlife religion, it must be able to address the curse of deep-seated and historic hostility.*

From the outset of his redemption project, God made it clear to Abraham that what he would accomplish through Abraham and his seed was intended for the whole world.* What God began with Abraham grew into a family, then into a tribe, and finally into a nation, kingdom, and culture. At the heart of the nation of Israel was their temple—the place where

---

* See Genesis 12:1–3.

the chosen people could encounter the living God. But Israel failed to live in covenant faithfulness with God. They broke covenant with God through idolatry and injustice. Despite the attempts of the prophets to turn Israel back to God, judgment finally fell in the form of destruction and exile. After the Babylonians destroyed the Jewish temple in Jerusalem in 586 B.C., the Hebrew prophets began to cast a vision for what a rebuilt and restored temple might look like. The prophet Isaiah envisioned a temple founded upon justice that would welcome foreigners (Gentiles).

> This is what the LORD says:
>   "Maintain justice
>   and do what is right,
>   for my salvation is close at hand
>   and my righteousness will soon be revealed...."
> Let no foreigner who has bound himself to the LORD
>   say,
>   "The LORD will surely exclude me from his
>   people."
> "...These I will bring to my holy mountain
>   and give them joy in my house of prayer.
>   Their burnt offerings and sacrifices
>   will be accepted on my altar;
>   for my house will be called
>   a house of prayer for all nations."
>   —ISAIAH 56:1, 3, 7, NIV

But Isaiah's vision of a justice and a Jewish temple that would accept foreigners was a minority report that was never implemented. By the time Herod the Great had completed his expansion of the rebuilt temple in Jerusalem around the time of Jesus's birth, the temple had become one of the architectural marvels of the Mediterranean world. Gentiles came from all over the Roman Empire to see Herod's temple. But Gentiles were prohibited from actually entering the holy precincts of the temple. Gentiles could observe as "tourists" but not participate as worshipers. So much for Isaiah's vision of a temple that would be a house of prayer for all nationalities! There was even a wall placed around the holy precincts of the temple with an inscription carved in stone every few feet. The inscription restricted Gentile access in no uncertain terms. Archeological remains of this dividing wall and its inscription have been found. The prohibiting inscription read:

> No foreigner is to go beyond this wall. Whoever is caught doing so will have himself to blame for his death, which will follow.

This was the *us* versus *them* divide set literally in stone. And it made it very clear how the Jews felt about the possibility of Gentiles joining them. *We're chosen, and you're not. We're in, and you're out. If you cross the line, we will kill you.* This is how the *us* versus *them* mentality usually plays out; it results in the erection of walls that engender hostility. The apostle Paul says this is the very thing that the cross of Christ destroys. Paul says the division, the alienation, the *us* versus *them* attitude— and even the very wall in the temple complex that created such hostility—are all removed through the cross.

> But now in Christ Jesus you who once were far off have been brought near by the blood of Christ. For he is our peace; in his flesh he has made both groups [Jews and Gentiles] into one and *has broken down the dividing wall, that is, the hostility between us.* He has abolished the law with its commandments and ordinances, that he might create in himself one new humanity in place of the two, thus making peace, and might reconcile

both groups to God in one body through the cross, thus putting to death that hostility [*"thereby killing the hostility,"* ESV].

—EPHESIANS 2:13–16, NRSV, EMPHASIS ADDED

The Kingdom of Heaven...on Earth

Paul presents the cross as the place where God ends human hostility and forms a new humanity—a new humanity capable of living together in peace. Paul then goes on, for the rest of the chapter, to talk about how Gentile believers in Messiah are now given full citizenship in the kingdom of God. Gentile believers are now joined to the Jewish saints. As Jesus had predicted, many Gentiles were coming from the east and west and sitting at the table of covenant with Abraham, Isaac, and Jacob, the Jewish patriarchs. This is the kingdom of heaven coming on earth.* Paul goes on to say that a new temple is now built upon the foundation of the Jewish apostles and Jewish prophets with the Jewish Messiah as the cornerstone. The whole purpose of this accomplishment is the establishment of peace.† This is all contained in the great mystery, which was given to the apostle Paul—the mystery of the acceptance of the Gentiles through the work of the Jewish Messiah.

In his similar letter to the Colossian church, Paul speaks of belief in Christ among the Gentiles as the hope of glory, which the prophets foretold.‡ It is because Gentiles can be joined to the God of Israel in Messiah that the prophetic hope of the knowledge of the glory of Yahweh covering the earth as the waters cover the sea can at last be fulfilled.§ Now, in Messiah, the chosen race is the *human* race, and the holy land is the *whole*

---

* See Matthew 8:11.
† See Ephesians 2:17–22.
‡ See Colossians 1:27.
§ See Habakkuk 2:14.

earth! This is the promise of God, the hope of the prophets, and the gospel of the apostles. This is God's plan, which was begun in Abraham, culminated in Christ, proclaimed by the apostles, and carried out by the church.

Paul understands that Jesus the Messiah has reformed, reframed, and redefined Israel in such a way that citizenship in the kingdom of God is no longer based upon the exclusive markers of ethnicity, circumcision, and Torah observance but upon the open-to-all possibilities of faith, baptism, and obedience to Messiah. Christ invites the whole world into the saving covenant. This is God's great work of egalitarian salvation. Not everyone can be an ethnic Jew. Not everyone can be circumcised (half of the population is excluded!). Not everyone can live in a culture adapted to Torah observance. But everyone can believe in Jesus as Messiah. Everyone can be baptized. Everyone can join the community of those committed to learning to live a life of obedience to Messiah. Jesus rescued the kingdom of God from ethnic, national, and cultural exclusivity. This was always the vision of God. This is the gospel—the good news. But not everyone saw the redefinition of the kingdom of God as good news.

> *Jesus rescued the kingdom of God from ethnic, national, and cultural exclusivity. This was always the vision of God. This is the gospel—the good news.*

One of the primary problems between Jesus and the Pharisees was the difference in their approaches to the *us* versus *them* attitude. While Jesus constantly challenged this attitude, the Pharisees tended to cherish it. It was religiously inspired hostility that the Pharisees cherished and Jesus challenged. This set Jesus and the Pharisees on an inevitable collision course. The Pharisees understood the kingdom of God as requiring the vigorous defense of the righteous *us* against the sinful *them*. Their interpretation of who was righteous and who was sinful was nonnegotiable—they were the righteous and those outside of their movement were the sinners. Black and white. Plain and simple. *Us* versus *them*.

In considering their approach to the *us* versus *them* divide, it is important to remember who the Pharisees were. The Pharisees were a conservative religious-political party who saw it as their mission to *take back Israel for God*. They attempted to do this by identifying, denouncing, and distancing themselves from those whom they perceived to be the sinners within society—the nonobservant (what we would call *secular* today) and the immoral. They specifically regarded tax collectors, prostitutes, adulterers, drunkards, Sabbath breakers, and other nonobservant Jews as the sinners who prevented the kingdom of God from coming in its fullness. The Pharisees were convinced that if they could convert a majority of the population to their movement, then God would send Messiah and restore Israel. Thus, the Pharisees saw those outside of their movement, those whom they identified as sinners, to be the reason why the full reign of God had not yet come to Israel. If they could ever produce a "moral majority" for the Pharisee party, at last the kingdom would come. Or so they thought.

Jesus's approach was the opposite. Jesus's practice was to welcome the very people alienated by the Pharisees. Jesus invited sinners to his table and offered them respect and forgiveness. Jesus called this practice *the kingdom of God*. Thus the battle lines were drawn between Jesus and the Pharisees. The fundamental disagreement was this—is the kingdom of God advanced through the *erection* or the *removal* of barriers? For the Pharisees, the kingdom of God would come when sinners were sufficiently marginalized within society. For Jesus, welcoming sinners to his table *was* the kingdom of God. For Jesus, the eradication of the *us* versus *them* attitude and the hostility it creates is a central ethic of the kingdom of God. Should the hostility between *us* versus *them* be enshrined or eradicated? The answer depends on whose approach to the kingdom of God you embrace—the approach of Jesus or the approach of the Pharisees.

It's no exaggeration to say that the Pharisees showed their faithfulness to God by hating the right people. No doubt they could produce scriptures to support their position of religiously endorsed hatred. For example, David says in the Psalms, "Do I not hate those who hate you, O Lord? And do I not loathe those who rise up against you? I hate them with complete hatred."*

The incredibly radical thing Jesus did was to dare to challenge conventional (and even scriptural!) concepts *based on his own authority*. So despite a scriptural endorsement for hating enemies, Jesus says, "You have heard that it was said, 'You shall love your neighbor and hate your enemy.' But I say to you, Love your enemies."† For the first-century Jew, the effect was the same as if a preacher stood up today and said, "The Bible says…but I say unto you…." Upon his own authority Jesus dared to countermand any scriptural endorsement for hating enemies. Instead of endorsing Moses or David, Jesus called for his disciples to love their enemies, and Jesus insisted that this alone is a mature imitation of our heavenly Father.‡

Yet as easy as it is to cast the Pharisees in the role of villains, I have some sympathy for them. Their encounter with Jesus and his radical teachings put them in a difficult position. They were going to have to make a very hard decision.

---

*   Psalm 139:21–22

†   Matthew 5:43–44

‡   See Matthew 5:43–48.

They were either going to remain true to their tradition and their understanding of the Scriptures—or they would have to rethink everything based on the new and radical teachings of a young carpenter turned rabbi from Nazareth. To abandon a centuries-old paradigm for a radical new vision of the kingdom of God would be no easy task. Make no mistake about it; what Jesus was teaching was new, radical, and utterly unprecedented. Jesus was teaching a kind of love that no one before had dared to imagine—love of enemy.

Jesus's radical vision of enemy-love presented a fundamental challenge to the religious view of the Pharisees. The Pharisees hated sinners because they loved God so much. Or so they thought. For them, the *us* versus *them* paradigm was religiously, even scripturally, mandated. Jesus challenged all of that. Jesus taught that we show how much we love God by how we love our enemies. This is the *seventy times seven* ethic taken to the extreme. Wayne Northey sums up Jesus's radical ethic of love like this: "The biblical test case for love of God is love of neighbour; the biblical test case for love of neighbour is love of enemy. Failure to love the enemy is failure to love God."[2]

When hating *your* enemy is understood as hating *God's* enemy is when the *us* versus *them* paradigm of hostility takes on a religious nature. Hating your enemy (who is believed to be the enemy of God) becomes a demonstration of your love for God. The stoning of an adulterous woman can be an act of piety—an act of piety with scriptural endorsement. The Pharisees could rightly say, "In the Law Moses commanded us to stone such women."*

Replacing Condemnation With Mercy

If the Bible says to stone adulterous women, shouldn't we stone them? Isn't this how the kingdom of God comes—by

---

* John 8:5

identifying, condemning, and punishing sinners? This is what the Pharisees believed. But Jesus challenged that. Jesus first responded by invalidating the Pharisees' *us* versus *them* divide. He did this by showing the Pharisees that they too were located within the category of sinners, that their cherished *us* versus *them* category was false and invalid. Jesus demolished their paradigm of hostility with his famous words, "Let him who is without sin among you be the first to throw a stone at her."* Jesus then replaced condemnation with mercy. Mercy triumphed over judgment. Jesus was the one who truly was without sin and who alone possessed the right to condemn (and throw the first stone!). But Jesus refused to condemn. Instead he forgave the woman and called her to a new life.

> *Make no mistake about it; what Jesus was teaching was new, radical, and utterly unprecedented. Jesus was teaching a kind of love that no one before had dared to imagine—love of enemy.*

Jesus challenged the cherished idea that a person can demonstrate how much they love God by how much they hate sinners and enemies. But unfortunately, the corrupt idea that you can prove your love for God by hating the right people lives on. It's the demonic philosophy of the suicide bomber. Political convictions alone do not produce a suicide bomber. The kind of hate that can produce a suicide bomber—hate of enemy that outweighs love of life—requires a religious element. The suicide bomber is deeply religious. The suicide bomber goes to his

---

* John 8:7

violent and murderous death with a prayer on his lips. The suicide bomber loves God. The suicide bomber shows how much he loves God by how deeply he hates. The suicide bomber loves God so much that he is willing to kill sinners and infidels on behalf of God and take his own life in the process. The suicide bomber loves by hating. The suicide bomber worships by hating. The suicide bomber gains heaven by hatred. The suicide bomber does what he does because he loves God. His God, The God he imagines. The God who is on his side. But this is not the God whom Jesus called Father.

Before we easily dismiss religiously endorsed hate as an exclusively Muslim problem, we must hasten to remind ourselves that, sadly, the *us* versus *them* attitude of religious hostility also has a Christian history. Religiously inspired hate not only gives birth to jihad and suicide bombers, but it is also responsible for giving the world the bloody legacy of the Crusades and Inquisitions. Tragically, the church has an undeniable history of endorsing and practicing violent hatred of enemies—ostensibly to prove love and devotion to God and to accomplish God's will. For nearly two hundred years (1095–1291) the Western church sanctioned a series of military campaigns against Muslims, usually with the misguided motive of "recovering the Holy Land." But the Crusades also unleashed the wanton slaughter of Jews and Greek Orthodox Christians.

During the Crusades era, popes and bishops preached impassioned sermons calling upon Christians to demonstrate their love for God by killing in the name of Christ and promising them heaven if they should die in the attempt. It doesn't make things any better when we understand that the various popes had political motives for launching their Crusades and simply used religious rhetoric to gain popular support. Indeed, skillful politicians know how to manipulate *us* versus *them* hostility for their purposes. Occasionally I encounter a Christian who attempts to defend the Crusades by arguing that the

Muslims were "just as bad or worse." But that is hardly the point, is it? The point is that we cannot call ourselves followers of the one who called us to love our enemies by killing them in his name. Swinging a sword underneath a banner of a cross may be the ultimate exercise in missing the point. The cross is where Christ forgives his enemies, not kills them.

The other bookend to the terror of the Crusades was the horror of the Inquisitions. During the Spanish Inquisition of the sixteenth century, tens of thousands of Jews were forcibly removed from Spain, and thousands of suspected heretics were tortured or burned at the stake. And lest Protestants feel their history is above the fray, we should remind ourselves that John Calvin defended the burning of the heretic theologian Michael Servetus in Geneva in 1553. Calvin justified the execution of heretics with this reasoning:

> There is no question here of man's authority; it is God who speaks and clear it is what law he will have kept in the Church, even to the end of the world. Where-fore does he demand of us a so extreme severity, if not to show us that due honour is not paid him, so long as we set not his service above every human consider-ation, so that we spare not kin nor blood of any, and forget all humanity when the matter is to combat for His glory.[3]

Calvin argued that God's "due honor" demands "extreme severity" and requires us to "forget all humanity" and "combat for his glory." And how does Calvin "combat for his glory"? By endorsing the execution of those who reject Christian theology. But the New Testament argues that God's glory was defended by the *cross* and that God was glorified when Jesus forgave his enemies from the cross.* Furthermore, Calvin defended

---

* See John 12:23–33.

the burning of heretics by imagining that this was "what law [God] would have kept in the Church." But the apostle James speaks of the royal law as loving your neighbor as yourself.* Quite bluntly, God's glory and God's honor are *not* defended by burning people at the stake. The church is built upon the shed blood of Christ, not the shed blood of heretics and infidels. Crusaders and inquisitors committed their atrocities in the name of "defending the faith." But what faith? Not the faith of Jesus. Not the faith of the apostles. Rather, it is the faith that justifies *us* versus *them* hostility in the name of God.

> *We cannot call ourselves followers of the one who called us to love our enemies by killing them in his name. Swinging a sword underneath a banner of a cross may be the ultimate exercise in missing the point. The cross is where Christ forgives his enemies, not kills them.*

Our Culture War Hostility

So much for history. What about today? What about the American evangelical church in the twenty-first century? Hopefully we are done with Crusades and Inquisitions, but do we still try to prove how much we love God and how faithful we are to God by how much hostility we hold toward certain groups? Secularists? Liberals? Homosexuals? Muslims? Or even toward other Christians whom we deem insufficiently orthodox? Is there an unspoken pressure to prove our righteousness by demonstrating a certain level of contempt toward these groups? Is there a kind of conservative Christian political correctness that requires a

---

* See James 2:8.

certain level of thinly veiled hostility? Have we embraced an "Ann Coulter Christianity" and made apostles of Rush, Beck, and Hannity instead of recognizing that they are simply entertainers and profiteers in America's culture war?

I fear that far too many followers of Christ have been sucked into the angry political polarization that characterizes our culture—a culture that has come to venerate the enraged rant as an art form. And when we do this, the name *Christian* is diminished to an adjective for modifying certain political positions rather than a noun for a person who is deliberately attempting to imitate Jesus Christ. This absolutely must change. We can hold all the convictions we want, as long as we can hold them in love. But we must take our culture war hostility to the cross and kill it!

For one thing, I'm not sure it is helpful to automatically identify secularists, homosexuals, and Muslims as enemies. But even if we do, the fact remains that Jesus calls us to love and bless our enemies, and not mock and revile them. Let's get this clear—loving the homosexual is no more an endorsement of homosexuality than Jesus's refusal to stone the adulterous woman was an endorsement of adultery. Because Jesus would not stone an adulterer did not mean Jesus was pro-adultery. Because Paul addressed the pagans of Athens respectfully did not mean Paul was pro-paganism. As we learn to sincerely love and respect secularists, homosexuals, and Muslims, it does not mean that we advocate secularism, support gay marriage, or endorse Islam. It simply means we are attempting to be authentic followers of Christ by granting everyone respect and dignity.

We must not be intimidated by the advocates of hostility who set up a false dichotomy and insinuate that a refusal to express animosity toward non-Christian groups is a *de facto* collusion with their position. Because Jesus did not practice the hostility of the Pharisees toward sinners, he was accused

of being a glutton and drunkard.* Of course, Jesus was neither.
Jesus simply refused the false notion that holiness can be demonstrated by hostility. A mistaken understanding of holiness
has a long history of getting mixed up with hostility.

> And in the distance the Jesus-lovers sat with hard con-
> demning faces and watched the sin.[4]

Thus John Steinbeck depicts the world-denying Pentecostals in *The Grapes of Wrath* as self-righteous, self-appointed
morality police who take perverse pleasure in condemning
the Saturday night square dance in the California migrant
camp. Steinbeck's terse portrayal of the "Jesus-lovers" is
unflattering but not an unfair invention of fiction. Unfortunately, such people do exist, and in their existence they hor
ribly distort the good news of Jesus Christ. The worst way
to define ourselves as Christian is in the negative—what
we are *against*. Steinbeck's migrant camp Jesus lovers were
against dancing (and most other expressions of humanness).
Of course, it is a caricature, but only in that it is perhaps an
exaggeration. Sadly though, there remains the misguided tendency to identify ourselves by what we condemn. And thus
the *us* versus *them* paradigm of religious hostility lives on.

I fear that through the cultivation of an *us* versus *them* attitude, we as evangelical Christians are communicating a subtle
(or at times not so subtle) hostility toward the wider culture.
The wider culture of "blue state America" is well aware that we
hold them in contempt. Ask a non-evangelical to define what
evangelicals believe, and odds are he or she will *not* speak in
terms of a personal salvation experience (the classical marker
of evangelicalism), but will give you a summary of political
positions and a list of cultural issues evangelicals are opposed
to. That these issues may indeed be real evils and not the

---

* See Matthew 11:19.

innocent dance of Steinbeck's novel is beside the point. The question remains: Do we really want to be primarily identified by what we are against? Do we want to be known for our angry voices and furrowed brows? Don't we have some good news to identify us? And at the heart of that good news don't we find the embracing message of acceptance and forgiveness?

Join the Dance of Humanness

Here are a few questions that are keys in overcoming an *us* versus *them* attitude and the hostility it breeds: What do we think of the world? Are we part of the world or not? Do we love the world or not? Do we have hope for the world or not? These questions throw us headlong into the controversy. There are Christians who would answer these questions with a thundering, *No! We're not part of the world, we don't love the world, and we have no hope for this doomed world!* But there are also Christians who would answer these questions with an enthusiastic, *Yes! We belong to this world, we love this world, and we have hope for God's good world.* So who's right? If we look to the Scriptures for guidance, as we should, things get interesting. The Bible's answer to these questions—*Do we belong to the world? Do we love the world? Is there hope for the world?*—is…yes and no. Consider these two well-known biblical passages from the same apostle.

> Do not love the world or the things in the world. If anyone loves the world, the love of the Father is not in him. For all that is in the world—the desires of the flesh and the desires of the eyes and pride in possessions— is not from the Father but is from the world. And the world is passing away along with its desires, but whoever does the will of God abides forever.
>
> —1 JOHN 2:15–17

> For God so loved the world, that he gave his only Son,
> that whoever believes in him should not perish but
> have eternal life. For God did not send his Son into
> the world to condemn the world, but in order that the
> world might be saved through him.
>   —JOHN 3:16–17

What's going on here? Are we supposed to love the world or
not? Is God condemning the world or not? Is the world passing
away or being saved? (And in case you are wondering, it's the
same Greek word—*kosmos*.) Herein lies the problem. Some
Christians are Epistle of John chapter 2 enthusiasts, while
others are Gospel of John chapter 3 adherents. The simple truth
is we must hold to both concepts of *kosmos*—we must learn
to live in the exquisite tension of John's dual use of *kosmos*.
So let me put it as simply as I can. The world as *a system of
rebellion against God* is corrupt and doomed. It is under the
judgment of God, and to love it is idolatry. This is the world
of Babylon. But the world as *God's creation and God's idea of
human society* is good and loved by God. This world is what
God intends to save. To love the world God created and to love
the good intention God has for human society is to cooperate
with God's redemptive purposes in Christ.

This is what the "Jesus-lovers" in *The Grapes of Wrath* (and
their contemporary ilk) have failed to understand. When Jesus
says, "For God so loved the world...", he does not simply mean
the individual people of the world. Jesus means that God loves
the very idea of human society. God is not simply interested
in saving parts of people ("souls") for an afterlife in heaven.
This kind of world-denying "gospel" is a gross distortion of the
life-affirming gospel that is found in the New Testament and is
always prone to foster the hostility of an *us* versus *them* divide.
God wants to salvage and reform (save and redeem) people,

and, in so doing, *save human society* or, as it is positively called by Jesus in John 3, "the world."

But do Steinbeck's "Jesus-lovers" who sit in judgment of the Saturday night square dance with their hard condemning faces really love the Jesus whose first miracle was to turn water into wine and keep the dance going? Jesus seems to be pro-dance. That is, Jesus endorses and participates in the celebration of humanness. In his birth and in his baptism, Jesus joined the human race. In his birth and in his baptism, Jesus transcended the *us* versus *them* divide, and in his crucifixion, Jesus killed the hostility that accompanies the *us* versus *them* attitude.

But does joining the dance of humanness have dangers? In some ways, yes. At times the line between the Babylon condemned by God and the Cana blessed by God is hard to distinguish. But to live as a world-denying, angry, judgmental separatist is such a betrayal of the logos, pathos, and ethos of Jesus as not to be an option. We must join the dance. As those who believe that God loves the world and is saving the world in Christ, we must joyfully belong to human society. We must join the dance. The church must creatively participate in the arts, music, poetry, literature, film, theater, athletics, education, entertainment, law, governance, business, finance, commerce, conservation, medicine, journalism, labor, science, research, philosophy, theology, and all that is necessary to produce a healthy, flourishing human society. We cannot sit with the pinched face world-deniers secretly hoping the worst will befall those who dare to try to enjoy life. Those who do so forfeit any claim of being filled with the love of Christ. We cannot present the face of Christ to a broken world with an angry scowl. An honest reading of the Gospels makes it clear that the only sin that regularly aroused Jesus's anger was the sin of self-righteous religiosity. We must not be found guilty of trying to turn people into the Ophelia of Bob Dylan's "Desolation Row."

Now Ophelia, she's 'neath the window
For her I feel so afraid
On her twenty-second birthday
She already is an old maid
To her, death is quite romantic
She wears an iron vest
Her profession's her religion
Her sin is her lifelessness
And though her eyes are fixed upon
Noah's great rainbow
She spends her time peeking
Into Desolation Row.[5]

John Steinbeck in *The Grapes of Wrath* and Bob Dylan in "Desolation Row" are both describing the same distortion of Christianity. An angry, world-denying, hostile, separatist, *us* versus *them* Christianity We must not be that way. Let us be neither *Grapes of Wrath* legalists nor "Desolation Row" religionists. Let's live and love God's good world! Let's embrace our shared humanity, join the dance, and be a part of God's mission to redeem his world. Redemption of the world requires, even demands, the eradication of groupthink hostility.

Paul says that at the cross Jesus killed the hostility. How does this work? Miroslav Volf explains it like this. "The open arms of Christ on the cross are a sign that God does not want to be without the other—humanity—and suffers humanity's violence in order to embrace it."[6] As human beings, we divide into our *us* versus *them* groups and foster hostility. We do so by imagining that the line separating good and evil runs between our respective groups. So that *we* are the good *us*, and *they* are the evil *them*. Such a division of good and evil is an illusion. The only legitimate good and evil divide between groups is the division between humanity and the Trinity. God—as the triune Father, Son, and Holy Spirit—is good, while humanity is evil. This is what Jesus is alluding to when he said, "Why do you call me good? No one is good except God alone."* The early church fathers were fond of describing the Trinity as a dance—an eternal dance of Father, Son, and Holy Spirit. A shared dance of mutual love and joy. Humanity is the alienated other. Humanity is outside the dance. But humanity is not just the other, but the beloved other, the beloved other who has become an enemy. As Miroslav Volf suggests, when God went forth to embrace his enemy, the result was the cross. But it is the cross that makes room for the embrace of reconciliation.

> *Let us be neither Grapes of Wrath legalists nor "Desolation Row" religionists. Let's live and love God's good world! Let's embrace our shared humanity, join the dance, and be a part of God's mission to redeem his world.*

In the most agonizing moment of the cross, known as the Cry of Dereliction, Jesus cried out, "My God, my God, why have you forsaken me?"† In that moment we might imagine a break occurring in the eternal dance of the Trinity, a momentary fissure *to make room for us.* Now humanity is invited to join with God in the joyful dance of reconciliation—a dance that not only celebrates reconciliation but also celebrates the death of hostility. When the Son prayed upon the cross, "Father, forgive *them*"—it was a plea to end the hostilities between us and them. The prayer our Savior prayed as he was being crucified forever defines how the Christ follower must regard the

---

* Mark 10:18
† Matthew 27:46

alienated *them*. Hostility is no longer permitted. As followers of Jesus Christ we must be willing to embrace the alienated *them* in forgiving love. This is how the hostility is killed, and this is how peace comes.

8

THE GOLDEN RULE AND THE NARROW GATE

THE SERMON ON the Mount is the largest single body of Jesus's teaching available to us. It is undeniably Jesus's most important sermon. It is the summation of what Jesus taught. It is his magnum opus. It is his grand treatise on how humans should live. The Sermon on the Mount is Jesus's defining statement concerning the nature of the kingdom of God. The Sermon on the Mount is Jesus's daring reformation of the Torah. Just as Moses from Mount Sinai delivered the law designed to form Israel into a just and worshiping society, so Jesus as the new Moses delivers a new law from a new mountain to re-form God's people in a new way.

The significance of the Sermon on the Mount cannot be overemphasized. The Sermon on the Mount is as important to understanding Jesus as the "Ninety-Five Theses" is to understanding Martin Luther or the "I Have a Dream" speech is to understanding Martin Luther King Jr. We cannot imagine trying to understand Luther apart from his "Ninety-Five Theses" or trying to understand Dr. King apart from his "I

Have a Dream" speech. Likewise it is impossible to understand Jesus apart from his Sermon on the Mount. But here is
the scandal: evangelical Christianity has tried to do just that—
has tried to understand Jesus apart from the Sermon on the
Mount!

I can say this because I have been around evangelical Christianity all my life, and the lack of emphasis on the Sermon on
the Mount is nothing short of scandalous. The Sermon on the
Mount is conspicuous by its absence in evangelical preaching,
writing, and thought. How is it that there are not countless
evangelical conferences and seminars and hundreds of evangelical books dedicated to understanding and living Jesus's
most important sermon? But there are not. And it is not merely
an oversight; it's a scandal.

Of course there is a reason why we avoid the Sermon on the
Mount. We are afraid of it. Its commands are daunting, and
its implications are enormous. Any serious attempt to actually *live* the Sermon on the Mount would require a profound
reevaluation of lifestyles and allegiances. And so we look for a
way out. We employ theologians to tell us how it doesn't mean
what it obviously means. We look for a way to tame the commands of Christ. A way to domesticate the Sermon on the
Mount. A way to painlessly accommodate the sermon to the
status quo. We try to marginalize the Sermon on the Mount.
We attempt to make the radical red letters of Matthew chap-
ters 5, 6, and 7 largely irrelevant to a very narrow definition of
salvation. Here is how we appeal to the theologians to "save"
us from the Sermon on the Mount: it's done by reducing salvation. ("Honey, I shrunk the gospel.")

Once we have reduced salvation and the purpose of Christ's
coming to "how to get to heaven when you die," the Sermon
on the Mount then seems marginal. And it must be marginalized, because if we're not outright afraid of the Sermon on
the Mount, we still run into the problem of how it doesn't fit

neatly into our evangelical "system" of salvation. The Sermon on the Mount is stubborn and unwieldy; it doesn't cooperate with a reductionist gospel concerned only with "how to get to heaven when you die." The Sermon on the Mount has no place in the *Roman Road* to salvation. The Sermon on the Mount lies outside the scope of the *Four Spiritual Laws*. And so, the Sermon on the Mount (Jesus's most important sermon!) goes either ignored or misread—or both.

Don't Compress the Gospel

Part of the problem lies with constricting the gospel to Good Friday and Easter Sunday. When we compress the gospel to the death and resurrection of Jesus, we make the life and teaching of Jesus largely superfluous. Thus we sum up Jesus's life and mission in catch phrases such as "he was born to die"—as if the only purpose of Jesus's life was to die on the cross. This is a tragic reduction and trivialization of the Incarnation. Certainly Jesus's life was such that it placed him on a trajectory with Calvary, and Jesus understood this from the beginning. But Jesus's life and ministry were not simply biding time until he died. We need to understand that the *whole* life of Christ is part of God's purpose to redeem the human race. As we come to understand the big picture of salvation, we must add Christmas theology to our Good Friday and Easter theology. Or to say it another way, the Incarnation is just as central to salvation as the Crucifixion and Resurrection.

When you begin with Bethlehem and not Calvary, you incorporate the Sermon on the Mount into the saving work of Jesus. Jesus was not just born to die; he was born to live—to live fully and freely, to live as no human had ever lived. Jesus was born to show humanity God's intention for human life and society. The grand purpose of the Incarnation is that God in Christ might join the human race. Why was this necessary? God joined the human race that he might give humanity a new start. God becomes human in Christ that humanity might be given a new Adam and a viable alternative to the dead end left to us in the old Adam. God joined the human race in Christ that he might not only command the way from on high, but also that he might *live* the way, *be* the way, *show* the way—the way to be truly and fully human. And Immanuel showed us the way *as one of us!* This is what Jesus is doing in the Sermon on the Mount, and it is massively important.

Greek Orthodox theology has always placed a much stronger emphasis on the role of the Incarnation in accomplishing salvation than either Roman Catholicism or Protestantism—an emphasis that gives us a much fuller and richer view of salvation. The great theologian of the Incarnation in the Orthodox Church is the fourth-century bishop Athanasius of Alexandria. In his seminal work on the Incarnation, Athanasius writes:

> You know what happens when a portrait that has been painted on a panel becomes obliterated through external stains. The artist does not throw away the panel, but the subject of the portrait has to come and sit for it again, and then the likeness is re-drawn on the same material. Even so was it with the All-holy Son of God. He, the Image of the Father, came and dwelt in our midst in order that He might renew mankind made after Himself.[1]

I love the analogy that the ancient saint gives us. Athanasius reminds us that God created humanity to bear his image, but the image of God in humanity has been stained and marred through sin. Yet God does not *throw away the panel.* God does not abandon his intention for humanity to bear his image. Instead the *subject* sits again so that the image might be repainted. This is the accomplishment of the Incarnation. And it's as we look at Jesus Christ that we remember what we are to look like, what we are to *be* like. Jesus Christ is a human as God intended. Jesus Christ is the one who faithfully bears the image of God and informs us how we should be.

> God joined the human race in Christ that he might not only command the way from on high, but also that he might **live** the way, **be** the way, **show** the way—the way to be truly and fully human.

This is why what Jesus is doing in the Sermon on the Mount is so vitally important. Jesus is teaching us and presenting us with the recovered image of God in humanity. Jesus is showing us how to be like God and how to bear God's image. And as we listen to the Sermon on the Mount, the recurring theme is forgiveness. *Blessed are the merciful. Turn the other cheek. Go the second mile. Give your cloak too. Love your enemies. Forgive as you are forgiven.* Then as Jesus begins to draw his great sermon to a conclusion, he says this:

> So whatever you wish that others would do to you, do also to them, for this is the Law and the Prophets. Enter by the narrow gate. For the gate is wide and the way is easy that leads to destruction, and those who enter by it are many. For the gate is narrow and the way is hard that leads to life, and those who find it are few.
>
> —MATTHEW 7:12–14

The Golden Rule and the narrow gate. These are two of the most memorable teachings from Jesus and his Sermon on the Mount. The Golden Rule is the command to treat others on the basis of how we want to be treated. The narrow gate is the difficult way that leads to life. The narrow gate is contrasted with the popular and easy way, which leads to destruction. But it is just here, with the Golden Rule and the narrow gate, that the scandal of the Sermon on the Mount is made abundantly clear. Even though these two concepts are spoken by Jesus in the same breath and are clearly connected in context, we have taken a crowbar to the Golden Rule and the narrow gate and tried to pry them apart as if they had nothing to do with one another. This is scandalous!

In much of evangelical thought, the Golden Rule has been reduced to a quaint platitude about being a nice person. Something from Mr. Rogers's neighborhood. As such, it has been banished to children's church, where it's used to teach kids how to "play nice." Meanwhile the narrow gate is somehow morphed into the sinner's prayer—the formula for how to get your ticket to heaven. So the narrow gate is a sinner's prayer, while the rigors of the Sermon on the Mount are left for those interested in extra credit. Wow. Not only is this bad biblical interpretation, but it also makes for bad Christianity. The text obviously reveals that the Golden Rule *is* the narrow gate! Jesus is saying, "Look, here is the summary of my sermon: treat others on the basis of how you want to be treated. Don't retaliate; forgive. This is the narrow gate. It's hard to do, but it's the road that leads to life." But we have not heard it that way. We've not taught it that way. We have taken a crowbar of horrendously poor biblical interpretation and tried to pry apart the Golden Rule and the narrow gate. Why? What is going on here?

This is what happens when we try to marginalize the Sermon on the Mount and shrink Christianity to a postmortem plan for going to heaven. The narrow way becomes a thirty-second sinner's prayer, and the rigors of the Sermon on the Mount are left for those who are interested in extra credit. But it won't work. For one thing, there is nothing hard about praying a sinner's prayer (it's exceedingly easy!). But Jesus specifically states that the narrow gate is something that is hard and difficult. Second, Jesus does not say this is the way to go to heaven when you die. This is not his topic in the Sermon on the Mount. Instead, Jesus is talking about how to live... *here and now*! Jesus is talking about a way of conduct that leads to life. Jesus is talking about an alternative way, which, though difficult, leads to life—the way of life that won't destroy us.

> *We have taken a crowbar to the Golden Rule and the narrow gate and tried to pry them apart as if they had nothing to do with one another. This is scandalous!*

Jesus teaches us that the way that seems right, the way that is easy, the popular way, the way in which we are scripted from birth, the way that most people go, is the *wrong* way. And in the end, it is the way that will ruin us. This idea is captured in a proverb, which I'm sure Jesus had in mind.

> There is a way that seems right to a person,
> But its end is the way of death.
> —PROVERBS 14:12, NRSV

The way that seems right is the way that is so pervasive, so popular, so assumed, so scripted by our culture, so endorsed by society that it seems to be the only way available. It is the way of the self-centered agenda. It is the way of getting ahead in life. It's the way of *looking out for number one.* This is the six-lane interstate highway of contemporary culture, which is presented to us in ten thousand commercials. *Drink our beer, drive our car, wear our watch, use our broker—and you'll be sexy, wealthy, cool, and happy!* As we travel the highway of consumerism, the signs all say we're on the road to happiness. But Jesus says the signs are a lie. Jesus says the bridge is out, and the way of self-seeking is the long road to ruin.

The way of prioritizing the pursuit of happiness is the way of the world; it's the way of Babylon. The way of *me first* is the way that seems right but ends in destruction. The way of basing motivation and decision making on *what I want* and *what's in it for me?* is the way of lust and pride—the lust of the flesh, the lust of the eyes, and pride in possessions.* As this plays out within society, it ends up to be largely a pursuit of money, sex, and power. The winners in a game where the score is kept on the basis of wealth, glamour, and influence are the celebrities on the covers of glossy magazines—they are the ones we look up to. They are the winners in the game. They are the most "successful" among us. There's nothing new about this. It was certainly the way of Caesar and Herod. But Jesus dares to challenge all of that. Jesus says the way of pursuing wealth, glamour, and influence based on prioritizing selfish interest and using others is *not* the way to live! In fact, Jesus says it is the way that leads to utter ruin and final destruction.

Salvation, as Jesus and the apostles taught it, is not a ticket to heaven but the kingdom of God. What Jesus tends to call the kingdom of God, Paul tends to call salvation; but they are both talking about the same thing. Our participation in the kingdom of God is our personal experience of salvation. Though there is the promise of being with the Lord in heaven

---

* See 1 John 2:16.

between our death and resurrection, this is never the emphasis. The emphasis is on how human beings and human society can be set right through the coming of the kingdom of God. What Jesus is doing in the Sermon on the Mount is teaching us how to live the kingdom of God. Jesus is teaching us how to live out our salvation.

Walking the Narrow Way by Living the Golden Rule

Instead of butchering the Sermon on the Mount by severing the Golden Rule from the narrow gate, let's do justice to what Jesus is teaching and see how the two go together—let's learn how to walk the narrow way by learning to live the Golden Rule. Or perhaps I could say it this way: What Jesus has joined together, let no man separate!

With this understanding, let's begin again—take it from the top and get an overview of Jesus's great sermon. Jesus begins the Sermon on the Mount with the deeply counterintuitive blessings of the Beatitudes.

> Blessed are the poor in spirit.
> Blessed are those who mourn.
> Blessed are the meek.
> Blessed are those who hunger and thirst for justice.
> Blessed are the merciful.
> Blessed are the pure in heart.
> Blessed are the peacemakers.
> Blessed are the persecuted.*

The Beatitudes are basically the exact opposite of what we are told in ten thousand commercials. The Beatitudes are so counter-intuitive and so contrary to our concept of what

---

* See Matthew 5:3-11.

constitutes a happy life that it would be easy to dismiss them as nothing more than naïve sentiment. The only reason we give them credence is that God has vindicated the teacher of the Beatitudes by raising him from the dead. Easter is many things, but among them Easter is God's endorsement of the Sermon on the Mount. Jesus lived his own sermon to the point of death, and God vindicated the veracity of the sermon by raising him from the dead!

The Beatitudes are not only counterintuitive; they are also subversive. Part of what the Beatitudes accomplish is to undermine the whole system of basing happiness on lust and pride—the mad pursuit of money, sex, and power. The Beatitudes challenge the basic value system of the fallen world order. As such the principalities and powers will always view the Beatitudes as a subversive threat to their rule—because they are! The Beatitudes constitute the core of Jesus's teaching. The remainder of the Sermon on the Mount is largely a commentary on the Beatitudes.

> To forgive is to give mercy instead of judgment, to give kindness instead of retaliation, to give pardon instead of punishment.

By the time we reach the Golden Rule and the narrow gate, Jesus is beginning to summarize his sermon. Jesus presents what we have come to call the Golden Rule with these words. "So whatever you wish that others would do to you, do also to them."* In using the word *so*, Jesus is connecting the Golden Rule with the previous passage. In the preceding five verses Jesus has been teaching us that God is a good father

---

* Matthew 7:12

who desires to give his children good things. As we connect the two passages, we see that what Jesus is teaching us in the Golden Rule is to imitate the goodness of our heavenly Father by giving good things to others.

And what shall we give? What do people want most of all from us? I'm going to suggest that what people want most of all is mercy. What people really want from us are kindness, mercy, and forgiveness. To "for-give" is to favorably give something. To forgive is to give mercy instead of judgment, to give kindness instead of retaliation, to give pardon instead of punishment.

Having given the mandate of the Golden Rule, Jesus then tells us that this is the grand summation of God's will as revealed in Scripture or, as Jesus says it, "for this is the Law and the Prophets." Very early in the Sermon on the Mount Jesus referenced the Law and Prophets when he said:

> Do not think I have come to abolish the Law or the Prophets; I have not come to abolish them but to fulfill them.
> —MATTHEW 5:17

What is meant by "the Law or the Prophets"? What does Jesus mean when he says that he did not come to abolish the Law or the Prophets, but to fulfill them? First let's consider the Law. The Torah of the Hebrew law is centered in the Decalogue—the Ten Commandments. We can summarize the Ten Commandments like this.

- No other gods.
- No idols.
- Don't presume with God's name.
- Keep the sacred day sacred.
- Honor your parents.
- Don't murder.

- Don't commit adultery.
- Don't steal.
- Don't lie.
- Don't envy.

The Ten Commandments were not merely dictates from God to regulate personal behavior—on a deeper level, the Ten Commandments were part of God's covenant with Israel. At Sinai God took Israel as his bride. God made covenantal promises to Israel, and as part of their covenant obligation, the Israelites were to observe the Ten Commandments as well as the entire Torah system, which developed around the Ten Commandments. The Torah was intended to keep Israel in covenant with God. Furthermore—and this is very important—the Torah was to form Israel into a just and worshiping society.

The first four of the Ten Commandments ordered Israel's relationship with God (worship), and the remaining six ordered Israel's relationship with others (justice). As Israel practiced the Law, they would be formed into a just and worshiping society. As a just and worshiping society, Israel would be blessed and would also be a blessing by becoming a light to the Gentiles. This was God's plan for Israel in the Law.

But as we know from our reading of Old Testament history, the people of Israel generally did not live up to their covenantal obligations. As Israel wandered away from covenant faithfulness and the faithful practice of the Ten Commandments, they encountered the ministry of the Prophets. The Hebrew prophetic tradition called Israel back into covenant faithfulness through actually *being* a just and worshiping society and not merely relying on their *status* as God's chosen people. This is what Isaiah, Jeremiah, and the rest were doing in their prophetic ministry. The Hebrew prophets pleaded with the Israelites to live up to their high calling by rejecting idolatry, immorality, and injustice—because idolatry, immorality, and injustice are the very opposite of what is produced through the observance of the Ten Commandments.

In the Sermon on the Mount, Jesus continues the Hebrew prophetic tradition by critiquing idolatry,[*] immorality,[†] and injustice.[‡] It is especially noteworthy that Jesus does not lessen the requirements of the Law, but in fact *raises* the standard. The prohibition on murder is expanded to a prohibition on anger. The prohibition on adultery is expanded to a prohibition on lust. The prohibition on taking the name of the Lord in vain is expanded to a prohibition on oaths altogether. Indeed, Jesus does not abolish the Law and the Prophets, but fulfills them. The idea that Jesus was a liberal reformer who was simply relaxing the standard of the Old Testament law as unattainable is a complete fabrication and a tragic misreading of the Gospels.

Later, when he was scrutinized by the Pharisees concerning his interpretation of the Torah, Jesus summarized the Law and the Prophets this way:

> You shall love the Lord your God with all your heart and with all your soul and with all your mind. This is the great and first commandment. And a second is like it: You shall love your neighbor as yourself. On these two commandments depend all the Law and the Prophets.
>
> —MATTHEW 22:37–40

Jesus is very clear about the fact that he did not come to abolish the Law and the Prophets, but to fulfill them. Jesus is not giving us a way out of fulfilling the commands to love God

---

* Matthew 6:19–24

† Matthew 5:27–30

‡ Matthew 6:1–4

and neighbor and still be saved; Jesus is giving us a way to live out salvation by actually loving God and neighbor. The coming of Messiah is not an abandonment of God's project with Israel; the coming of Messiah is the fulfillment and expansion of God's project with Israel. God's plan to form a just and worshiping society is not abandoned with the coming of Messiah; it is fulfilled with the coming of Messiah.

There has long been an unspoken idea, a half-baked notion, that God began something with Israel and then found out it wouldn't work, so he scrapped it for a different plan with Jesus. This is terrible biblical interpretation, and it flies in the face of everything taught in the Gospels and epistles. Jesus is not "Plan B." God doesn't have a Plan B. God's plans don't fail. God has always had one plan—a plan that began in Abraham, continued with Israel, culminated in Christ, and is carried on by the church. It is God's single plan to form a just and worshiping society through a reconstituted Israel, which will bring light and healing to the nations.

In the Sermon on the Mount, Jesus is showing us what a true son of Abraham looks like. Jesus is showing us what Moses was trying to build all along. Jesus is showing us how Isaiah's dreams can come true. Jesus is showing us how a true follower of Messiah is to live. But Jesus doesn't merely teach us or even just set an example—though he does both of these things. Jesus invites us to believe in him, and in so doing to connect our lives to him so that his life enables us to fulfill the vision set forth in the Law and the Prophets. When this happens, this is what Jesus calls *fruit*. In John chapter 15 Jesus speaks of himself as the vine and his disciples who believe in him as the branches. As these believing branches draw their life from Messiah, they produce the fruit intended by the Law and the Prophets—the fruit of love for God and neighbor.

Producing the Fruit of Love

Somewhere along the way in our post-Reformation paranoia of anything that references works—a paranoia not endorsed by the New Testament—we have distorted salvation. The salvation of Messiah that *fulfills* the Law and the Prophets becomes salvation *from* fulfilling the Law and the Prophets. And the results have been disastrous. To put it more bluntly—we have invented a Christianity where the Golden Rule and the narrow gate are utterly disassociated ideas. But once we pry apart the Golden Rule and the narrow gate, we have concocted a distorted Christianity that is self-centered, that is afterlife oriented, and that abolishes the Law and the Prophets—the very thing Jesus said he did *not* come to do!

So immediately after introducing the Golden Rule as the narrow gate, Jesus talks about how a tree is judged by its fruit.* Then Jesus exposes the danger of prioritizing miracles over works of mercy and justice.† Finally Jesus concludes his great sermon with the parable of two houses—one built upon the rock and one built upon the sand.‡ Jesus is saying that those who hear the Sermon on the Mount and its call to radical forgiveness, and choose to live according to Messiah's mandate, are building upon a foundation that will endure the coming storms. Likewise, those who hear the Sermon on the Mount but choose to live according to the old way of nonforgiveness and violent resistance are doomed to destruction.

It should be noted that this was not just a nice, timeless illustration with which to close a sermon. Jesus's closing parable of the two houses is prophetic and has a historic fulfillment. It was the old way of nonforgiveness and violent resistance that produced the Jewish rebellion against Rome and led to the

---

* Matthew 7:15–20

† Matthew 7:21–23

‡ Matthew 7:24–27

destruction of Jerusalem and its temple a generation later. At the same time that the house built upon the sand (the Jewish temple) was being destroyed, the apostles were laying the foundation for a new temple made of living stones with Christ Jesus as the cornerstone. This is the house that would not fall because it had been founded upon the rock.

> *But once we pry apart the Golden Rule and the narrow gate, we have concocted a distorted Christianity that is self-centered, that is afterlife oriented, and that abolishes the Law and the Prophets—the very thing Jesus said he did **not** come to do!*

From this lesson we should learn that a good way to secure the fall of Christianity is to separate the Golden Rule from the narrow gate. A good way to ruin Christianity would be to misread the apostle Paul in such a way that the Sermon on the Mount is marginalized and made largely irrelevant to the way of salvation. A good way to cheapen the gospel and make it largely irrelevant to contemporary society is to reduce salvation to what happens when you die, thus making salvation a postmortem issue that can be taken care of in a thirty-second prayer. A good way to guarantee that Christianity becomes a withered tree without fruit is to marginalize Jesus's teaching about enemy-love and radical forgiveness and suggest that these are optional for those interested in extra credit, but certainly not central to God's program of salvation. This is the very thing our best teachers and theologians have said we must not do!

To claim the comfort of the Crucified while rejecting his way is to advocate not only cheap grace but a deceitful ideology.[2]

Christ's teaching and Christ's death on the Cross are not two separate issues. Christ's *way*, the narrow path, is the road of loving and forgiving even unto death. And He didn't say, "Let me do that for you." He said, "Come die with me."[3]

To confess and testify to the truth as it is in Jesus, and at the same time to love the enemies of that truth, his enemies and ours, and to love them with the infinite love of Jesus Christ, is indeed a narrow way.[4]

"Whatever you wish that others would do to you, do also to them." This is the Golden Rule and the narrow gate. And to live out the Golden Rule and thus fulfill the Law and the Prophets requires a very specific exercise—you must confer humanity upon others and consider what it is like to be them. This is not always easy. By definition, *them* is the other, the one or ones who are not *us*. To obey what Jesus is teaching us, we must be willing to actively think and imagine what it would be like to be in the place of the other—to be them. This is especially true when the *them* we are called to relate to occupy the role of enemy.

As Christians we tend to regard certain groups of people as enemies to the Christian faith. Even if as individuals they are not an enemy to the Christian faith, we may regard their religion, their worldview, their lifestyle, their politics to be contrary to Christian conviction, and thus a kind of enemy. So how shall we treat them? To answer the question, we must first consider what it would be like to be them. What would it be like to be an atheist, a radical secularist, gay, Muslim? And how would we like to be treated by the Christian community? I think the only suitable answer is that we would like to be treated with dignity and respect. But as long as we demonize and dehumanize *them*, it is impossible to live out the Golden Rule. It is entirely possible to disagree with *them* and still love and respect *them*. This is the Christlike way—this is the narrow gate.

The narrow gate is not the way of narrow-minded bigotry. The narrow way is the Christlike way where we must consistently treat others with respect and dignity—even if they treat us with disrespect and contempt. For a Christ follower, the antagonistic attitude of *us versus them* collapses once we enter the narrow gate.

Occasionally I'm asked to join some online group with a name like *Christian and proud of it*. I always decline. You can be *a* Christian—in the sense of *status*—and be proud of it. But you cannot be Christian—in the sense of *Christlike*—and cultivate an attitude of antagonistic pride. I'm afraid that too much of what we have considered "standing up for Jesus" has really been in-your-face antagonism. Do we need to fly the flag of Christian cultural identity as much as we need an emphasis on the cultivation of Christlike character?

Being Christlike in a Caesar-like World

In the current vitriolic and polarizing culture-war atmosphere, a Sermon on the Mount emphasis of giving mercy, going the second mile, turning the other cheek, and forgiving "seventy times seven" would serve the cause of Christ far better than an angry stance that smacks of *we're Christians and we're not going to take it anymore*. Jesus said his disciples would be known for their love, not for their placards of protest and angry letters to the editor. The angry rhetoric of retaliation may be cathartic, but it's not Christlike.

Recently I was at a stoplight, and the car in front of me had a bumper sticker that read: "I like your Christ. I do not like your Christians. They are so unlike your Christ." The statement is attributed to Mahatma Gandhi. Of course it's overstated and far too much of a glaring generalization. But I find little comfort in that. When I saw that bumper sticker, I wanted to get out my car, walk up to the driver, and...apologize. I wanted to say something like, "I know. We have been far too unlike our Christ. Please forgive us."

> The narrow gate is not the way of narrow-minded bigotry. The narrow way is the Christlike way where we must consistently treat others with respect and dignity—even if they treat us with disrespect and contempt.

There is a place for Christian apologetics. There is also a place for Christian apology. There is a place for vigorously defending the Christian faith with intelligent, reasoned debate. There is also a place for simply loving the enemy of the Christian faith and trusting God to defend the truth. Not every attack upon the Christian faith needs a response, and no attack upon the Christian faith needs an angry, threatening response. Forgiveness is a kind of Christian suffering, and sometimes we are simply called to suffer.

> For to this you have been called, because Christ also suffered for you, leaving you an example, so that you might follow in his steps. He committed no sin, neither was deceit found in his mouth. When he was reviled, he did not revile in return; when he suffered,

> he did not threaten, but continued entrusting himself
> to him who judges justly.
>
> —1 PETER 2:21–23

We live in a world where much is wrong. And what is most wrong with the world is not the politics or the economy or who happens to be living in the White House. What is most wrong with the world is the human heart. The greed and pride and lust of the human heart are the epicenter of all that is wrong with the world. We should realize this by now. As followers of Christ, we are not so much called to know the answer or preach the answer as much as we are called to *be* the answer. This is how we are salt and light (also found in the Sermon on the Mount). We are to model the answer by being Christlike in a Caesar-like world. This is what the Sermon on the Mount is all about.

The simple fact that what is most wrong with the world is the condition of the human heart is why the world can never be changed by politics alone. Never! The sooner we have less faith in the capacity of politics to effect the change we are commissioned to bring about, the better. What is needed is less faith in politics and protest, and more faith in the power of the gospel to change the world by transforming hearts. This is why Jesus didn't commission his disciples to run for office, but to walk in his ways. Jesus didn't commission his disciples to campaign for a new Caesar, but to proclaim a new birth. Jesus commissioned twelve apostles, not twelve politicians. Do we really think if we just get enough elephants or donkeys (or whatever team mascot we cheer for) in Washington we will transform the nation? This is not the method of Jesus or the apostles. It's not about getting the right number of Rs or Ds in Congress, but about changing the hearts of both Rs and Ds. We are not called to follow an elephant or a donkey; we're called to follow a Lamb! (Which doesn't mean we should form a Lamb political party!) It means we should first model the way of the Lamb and then make disciples of both elephants and donkeys in the way of the Lamb. And the way of the Lamb is above all things the way of extending radical forgiveness and considering others in love.

The narrow (and difficult) way of the Golden Rule demands that we *consider* and not *use* others. The Golden Rule of considering others by giving them love, respect, and mercy is the narrow gate that leads to salvation. Not because this is how salvation is *earned*, but because this is how salvation is *lived*. It is the broad and popular way of using others that is the very way we ruin our souls. Using other people as objects to satisfy our self-centered agenda is absolutely the highway to hell—it is the kind of life that leads to the utter and final ruin of the human soul. When creatures created in the image of God cooperate with sin and Satan to use other image-bearing creatures as objects to satisfy their own greed and lust, they conspire to erase the image of God from their own soul. This is what Jesus is trying to save us from in teaching us the narrow way of the Golden Rule.

Whether it is a girl on the other side of town used to satisfy lust for sex, or a child on the other side of the world used to satisfy greed for cheap shoes, such use of people is prohibited by the Golden Rule. It is prohibited not only because it destroys the people whom we use as objects to satisfy our lust for money, sex, and power, but also because it is the very process that ruins our own soul. Jesus is trying to save us from ruining our souls! Jesus is not giving us a means of walking the broad road of lust, pride, and greed and still be saved; rather Jesus is calling us to follow him on the narrow road that leads to life. The idea that tickets to heaven can be handed out to people committed to walking the broad road to destruction is a diabolical fantasy. Salvation is not a ticket. Salvation is a road. It is a road where Jesus is the way, the truth, and life.

Salvation is a life to be lived. Salvation is a life of following Jesus as the way, looking to Jesus as the truth, imitating Jesus as the life worth living. When we live this way because of our faith response to Jesus Christ, we are *in* the way of salvation.

> *The Golden Rule of considering others by giving them love, respect, and mercy is the narrow gate that leads to salvation. Not because this is how salvation is earned, but because this is how salvation is lived.*

This is the Sermon on the Mount—to choose the Christlike way of giving over the Caesar-like way of taking. To give mercy to the undeserving. To forgive the offender. To turn the other cheek to the enemy. To go the extra mile with the oppressor. To give the cloak to the scoundrel. To give cheerfully to the beggar. To forgive again and again. Seventy times seven. This is the narrow way that Christ invites us to follow him on. It is a hard and difficult way. But because it is Christ who invites us to follow, it is also possible.

Above all, it is the way that leads to life. Do we dare believe this? Do we dare believe that this hard and difficult way that looks like losing and dying is, in fact, the way that leads to life and salvation? To be Christians means that we do believe this. And not only do we believe it; we live it. But we don't live it alone. We can't live it alone. We live it in community with others who share our faith in Jesus Christ. Even more significantly, we live it in fellowship with the One who promised to never leave us or forsake us and to be with us on the narrow road to the end of the age.

9

BEAUTY WILL SAVE THE WORLD

N THEIR INTELLIGENT song "Philosophia," the Irish band Guggenheim Grotto sings about the human capacity to recognize beauty and the desire we all have for our lives to be beautiful—for our lives to be a work of art. The song rejects the idea that in any ultimate sense beauty is relative.

> When we're young we set our hearts upon some
> beautiful idea
> Maybe something from a holy book or French
> philosophia
> Upon the thoughts of better men than us we swear by
> and decree a
> Perfect way to end the war of ways the only way to be
> a work of art
> Oh, to be a work of art.
>
> But in time a thought comes tugging on the sleeve
> edge of our minds
> Perhaps no perfect way exists at all, just many
> different kinds

> Oh but if it's just a thing of taste then everything
>   unwinds
> For without an absolute how can the absolute define
> A work of art?
> Oh, to be a work of art.[1]

We humans recognize that there is something definitive and absolute about beauty. Like our sense of justice, we seem to be born with an instinct to recognize beauty. Of course there is plenty of room for variation in taste, but beauty itself is an absolute. No one looks at a majestic sunset or a snowcapped mountain range and thinks these vistas are ugly. We universally recognize such scenes as absolutely beautiful. There exists within our hearts some absolute standard for beauty, just as there exists in our hearts some absolute standard for justice. We relate to beauty the same way we relate to justice—as an intuitive recognition of absolutes.

Our instincts for justice and beauty (conscience and aesthetics) are a deep problem for the atheist. Our consciences, our instinct for justice, bear witness to the existence of a transcendent lawgiver. Likewise, our instinctual appreciation for beauty seems to bear witness to the existence of an ultimate artist. The pursuit of justice and the pursuit of beauty lead us to the supreme judge and the paramount artist.

It is a sense of justice as an absolute that tells us that abusing children is always morally wrong. But where does this absolute sense of justice come from? Inevitably the answer to this question leads us to God. There is no way around it. There is no supreme law without a supreme lawgiver. As Fyodor Dostoevsky observes in *The Brothers Karamazov*, without God all things are permissible.[2] Likewise, some absolute sense of the artistic tells us that Vincent Van Gogh's *Starry Night* or Rembrandt's *Return of the Prodigal Son* is beautiful. But I would argue that without God, nothing can be said to be beautiful or ugly. As the song lyric says: "For without an absolute how can the absolute define a work of art?" The Christian explanation for the human capacity to recognize justice and beauty is this: we are created in the image of God, and as such we share God's passion for justice and beauty.

> Out of Zion, the perfection of beauty,
> God shines forth.
> —PSALM 50:2

Beauty Will Save the World

In Fyodor Dostoevsky's classic novel *The Idiot*, the Christlike character of Prince Myshkin makes this peculiar statement. "Beauty will save the world."[3] This mysterious phrase has fascinated Christian thinkers and theologians ever since and has inspired scores of papers, essays, and lectures on what it might mean. Aleksandr Solzhenitsyn in his Nobel Lecture on Literature said this about it:

> Dostoevsky's remark, "Beauty will save the world,"
> was not a careless phrase but a prophecy.[4]

I agree with Solzhenitsyn. There is no doubt that Fyodor Dostoevsky was a prophet who foresaw much. Not only did the great Russian writer foreshadow the demonic mentality that would characterize the Bolshevik Revolution and Communist Russia in his disturbing novel *Demons*, but Dostoevsky also seems to have had a powerful grasp on the nature of how God saves the world through Christ. In his simple phrase "Beauty will save the world," Dostoevsky gives us a prophetic perspective on the relationship between beauty and the saving grace of forgiveness. Beauty is not just an embellishment of God's creation, but it is beauty that will save the world.

Over the past few years I have made a conscious attempt to cultivate a greater awareness and deeper appreciation for beauty. Whether I'm hiking in the mountains or simply driving to work on a beautiful spring morning, I am attempting to train my eye to recognize and appreciate beauty wherever I encounter it. I'm convinced this is a vital aspect of spiritual growth and development. To notice and appreciate beauty is a spiritual discipline—it is a holy act—beholding the beauty of God's creation is an aspect of worship.

The appreciation of beauty is part of our unique task as humans. God is an artist, and as an artist God has not created a merely utilitarian universe but a universe full of wondrous beauty. God has endowed humans with the capacity to create, recognize, and appreciate beauty. As every artist desires that his creative work be recognized and appreciated, so it is that when we recognize and appreciate the beauty in God's handiwork, we are engaging in a kind of worship.

Etty Hillesum was a Jewish thinker and spiritual mystic from Holland who died at the age of twenty-nine at the infamous Nazi death camp in Auschwitz, Poland. During her months at Auschwitz, Etty kept a diary. In it she wrote:

> Sometimes when I stand in some corner of the camp, my feet planted on Your earth, my eyes raised toward Your heaven, tears sometimes run down my face, tears of deep emotion and gratitude....And I want to be there right in the thick of what people call "horror" and still be able to say: life is beautiful. And now I lie here in a corner, dizzy and feverish and unable to do a thing....But I am also with the jasmine and with that piece of sky beyond my window....For once you have begun to walk with God, you need only keep on walking with Him and all of life becomes one long stroll—such a marvelous feeling.[5]

For Etty Hillesum, the memory of jasmine and a glimpse of the sky—even at Auschwitz—was enough to remind her that life is beautiful and to evoke in her a deep sense of worship! If ever there was a hell on earth, surely it was Auschwitz. Yet Etty Hillesum testified that she was able to find beauty and worship the Creator of that beauty...even amidst the horrors of Auschwitz. Such capacity to find God in even the most hellish of places reminds me of these words of David: "If I make my bed in hell, behold, You are there."* Wherever we find the footsteps and fingerprints of God, there we find beauty.

But beauty far too often goes unrecognized. There is something tragically profane about our technological society if it blinds us to the beauty of creation—something profane, dehumanizing, and denigrating. We must not allow cubicles, computer screens, and the maddening pace of modern life to distract us from the important task of marveling at the beauty God creates day by day. There is an ambient beauty, which we must perceive and not allow the devil to steal from us. This beauty is all around us. The beauty in the prologue of sunrise and the epilogue of sunset. The daily drama of the clouds. The ocean with its many moods. The quiet beauty of trees in full leaf or the poignant beauty of gently falling snow. If we fail to see these beautiful moments and fail to recognize them as the artistic achievements of God, we fail in one of our essential tasks as human beings.

I remember climbing the twin summits of Desolation Peaks in Rocky Mountain National Park with one of my sons, and being the only two people on the mountain that particular day. I told my son that the grandeur and majesty of those twin peaks needed to be appreciated, and that this day it was our task and our privilege to do so. We understood that to climb a mountain with conscious wonder and genuine appreciation

---

*   Psalm 139:8, NKJV

for the beauty of God's creation was not only a physical act of recreation but also a spiritual act of worship.

Along with an awareness of natural beauty, my wife and I actively cultivate an appreciation for artistic beauty. As we travel, we take time to visit art galleries and museums. Why? Because, like the prophets, artists are seers. The artist is a seer who perceives the spiritual world beyond the material veil. The best poets and painters and writers and musicians are agents of God's grace. These artists do holy work as they interpret the world through revelation and help create beauty. Artists give us a deeper view of the world around us—a view beyond that of crass, soulless materialism. Artists who create beauty help deliver us from the all too present curse of pragmatism.

Ours is a pragmatic age, and we are the spiritually poorer for it. Pragmatism as a worldview is a distortion of God's creation. Pragmatism is a kind of vandalism. Pragmatism sees creation as a commodity to be used—it assigns value on the basis of how a thing can be "made useful." Pragmatism is a spiritual blindness, a blindness that misses much of the value of beauty because beauty isn't "useful" in any utilitarian sense. Beauty belongs to those things that, though not necessary for survival, are necessary to make survival worth the effort. God's world is full of "impractical" beauty, but pragmatism has little use for beauty (unless it can be bought and sold!). Beauty is not pragmatic—beauty is *holy*! Beauty is holy because all beauty is ultimately some expression of the glory of God. As Abraham Joshua Heschel has said, "Beauty and grandeur are not anonymous; they are outbursts of God's kindness."[6]

Heschel's observation is profound and true. An encounter with beauty is an encounter with the glory of God. This is why beauty, though universally recognized (at least by a soul not dehumanized through pragmatism), remains so hard to define.

The Merriam-Webster dictionary defines *beauty* as "a combination of qualities, such as shape, color, or form, that pleases the aesthetic senses." Well, yes, I suppose beauty is that too. But it is much, much more than that. I would rather say that beauty is a glimpse of the glory of God.

> In Christ, the affliction of the crucifixion becomes the beauty of forgiving grace.

Because beauty belongs to the glory of God, it speaks to the deepest part of our being. Simone Weil was right when she taught us that beauty and affliction are the only two things that can pierce our heart. And it is these two piercing realities—affliction and beauty—that come together at Calvary. In Christ, the affliction of the crucifixion becomes the beauty of forgiving grace. This is the beauty that saves the world, which Dostoevsky hinted at. It is the paradoxical beauty of the cross. The cross is where human ugliness is swallowed by the beauty of forgiving love in a collision of sin and grace.

The central mystery of Christianity is the Incarnation, and the mystery of the Incarnation encounters its deepest paradox at the cross, for the cross is where nothing is as it appears!

The cross appears to be a failure. It was an accepted truism that a crucified messiah was a failed messiah. Yet the cross is nothing less than the victory of God.

The cross appears to be the ultimate rejection. At the cross, Jesus of Nazareth is rejected by both the nation of Israel and the Roman Empire. Yet the cross is where God reconciles the world unto himself.

The cross appears to be a senseless tragedy. A promising young man in his early thirties is falsely accused, wrongly convicted, and shamefully executed. Yet the cross is where all tragedy must be reinterpreted in light of resurrection.

The cross appears to be ugly. Crucifixion was not just ugly; it was ghastly. Crucifixion was a Roman weapon of terror intended to intimidate an occupied populace. Yet the cross has become—and I mean this quite literally—*the most beautiful thing in the world!*

You may be tempted to dismiss my claim as religious hyperbole, but I stand by it: *the cross is the most beautiful thing in the world.* The cross is the beauty that saves the world. When Jesus, upon the cross, prayed, "Father, forgive them," we encounter the beauty of cruciform love. (*Cruciform* means "a cross-shaped form.") The proper term in describing the beauty of the cross is *exquisite.* Exquisite beauty is beauty so intense that it is felt as a kind of agony. And that is what we encounter at the cross—an agony of beauty. The cross is where the greatest beauty emerges in the midst of the greatest ugliness. And it is from that beauty that God intends to save the world. This is our gospel.

Our gospel tells a beautiful story. It goes like this. In the beginning, God created the heavens and the earth. God's creation was good. Through sin the world went wrong. At the cross, God brought an end to sin and re-created his universe according to forgiving love. At the cross we find the exquisite beauty of God absorbing the ugliness of sin and giving nothing in return but forgiving love. The cross is man at his worst and God at his best. But the cross is also man at his best. As the Son of Man, Jesus recovers through his obedience what Adam (mankind) had lost through disobedience. So we can truly say that the best of God and the best of man meet together in Christ at the cross. The cross is where the beauty of reconciliation happens—and nothing is more beautiful than the reconciling love of God at Calvary. Paul explains it like this: "In Christ God was reconciling the world to himself, not counting their trespasses against them."* At the cross, raw hate and violence are turned into pure love and forgiveness with the words, "Father, forgive them." This is beautiful beyond telling.

Yet we must tell it, or at least try to tell it. And this is where the artists can help us. I used to see beautiful artistic depictions of the Crucifixion and not understand what the artists were doing. I would think: *Why do artists paint the Crucifixion like that? It's so unrealistic. Don't they know the Crucifixion wasn't like that?* But now I realize that the artists knew more than I did. Of course the artists knew that what they were doing was not an exercise in realism—what they were doing was an exercise in *revelation*. The artists aren't trying to give us a reenactment; they are trying to give us understanding. We don't need a realistic depiction of the cross; we need a revelation of the cross. Art has the capacity to transport us from the constricted realm of realism into the expansive realm of revelation. If we had a journalistic photograph of the crucifixion of Christ, it would not be beautiful; it would be ghastly. If we looked at it once, I suppose we could never bear to look at it again. There would be no *apparent* beauty in the photograph. But the reverent artist knows that beauty *is* there. The exquisite beauty of love and forgiveness is eternally alive at the cross—the exquisite beauty of cruciform love.

This is why the artistic depictions of the Crucifixion by the great masters have the capacity to speak to us so powerfully—they transcend realism and help usher us into the realm of revelation. When I look at the famous painting *The Crucifixion* by the Renaissance artist Andrea Mantegna (now hanging in the Louvre in Paris), I see exquisite beauty. The agony is present, but the beauty is undeniable. When I saw the painted crucifix at the San Damiano chapel in Italy, I understood how it could

---

* 2 Corinthians 5:19

speak to a young Francis of Assisi and transform his life. The
San Damiano crucifix seems to radiate love—a beautiful love
that can save the world. For me none of the artistic depictions of the Crucifixion are more beautiful than the fresco of
The Crucified Christ by the Renaissance monk and artist Fra
Angelico. When I look at Fra Angelico's masterpiece, I feel as
if I am seeing pure cruciform love.

> *We now understand the suffering and death
> of Christ, not merely as brutal violence leading
> to a cruel execution, but as the beautiful
> act of self-giving love and transforming
> forgiveness that saves the world.*

As I write this chapter, I have a Russian Orthodox cross
icon sitting on the table where I am working. It has been hand
painted with painstaking detail. It depicts five events from the
passion narrative—Jesus carrying his cross, his crucifixion,
Jesus's body being taken down from the cross, his burial, and
his resurrection. Four of those events, if depicted in utter
realism, would be images of horrific violence and a gruesome
death, yet the entire icon is a thing of beauty, a work of art.
Why? Because all of the events are now informed and transformed by the resurrection of Jesus Christ. We now understand the suffering and death of Christ, not merely as brutal
violence leading to a cruel execution, but as the beautiful act
of self-giving love and transforming forgiveness that saves the
world. The images I see on the icon are that of evil being overcome by good, of hate being conquered by love, of vengeance
being absorbed by forgiveness, of death being swallowed by

life. The cross icon I see before me is a depiction of the beauty that saves the world.

Andrea Mantegna, Fra Angelico, and countless other artists throughout Christian history have artistically interpreted the Crucifixion in terms of beauty. These artists know the Crucifixion didn't *look* beautiful but that it *was* beautiful. It was the beautiful act of forgiveness. Is there anything more beautiful than an act of undeserved forgiveness seeking reconciliation? I don't think so. This is the beauty we find in the father's embrace of the prodigal son. It is why it is such a fitting subject for a Rembrandt masterpiece.

Centered at the Cross

The Dutch theologian Henri Nouwen once spent an entire day seated in front of Rembrandt's *Return of the Prodigal Son* in the Hermitage Museum in St. Petersburg, Russia, and wrote a book on how the painting changed his life and transformed his view of Christianity. Radical forgiveness seeking reconciliation truly is the beauty of Christianity. The great Swiss theologian Hans Urs von Balthasar said:

> Being disguised under the disfigurement of an ugly crucifixion and death, the Christ upon the cross is paradoxically the clearest revelation of who God is.[7]

Hans Urs von Balthasar is right about the cross being the clearest revelation of who God is. The cross takes us to the very core of God's nature. This is why our reading of Scripture must be centered at the cross. The Bible is a big book covering the long and complicated history of God's involvement with humanity. It is possible to derive varying and even contradictory ideas of the nature of God from a selective reading of the Bible! As an example, I assume most of us would not regard the command of God for the Israelites to slaughter Canaanite women and children as the clearest revelation of who God is. So where shall we center our reading of Scripture? Where is the touchstone? What is the definitive lens for interpretation? Where shall we point to in Scripture and say, "There is God! That is what God is like!"? I agree with Hans Urs von Balthasar that it is the cross. It is in the ugly brutality of crucifixion that the beauty of God's love is most clearly revealed.

Of all the possible ways of understanding the nature of God, I insist that none is more complete than when we see Jesus Christ hanging upon the cross with his arms outstretched in a loving embrace of the whole world—an embrace that included his enemies. To understand God best, we should look to Christ upon the cross forgiving a world that has rejected him. This is the love that saves us. The apostle John famously tells us that God is love.*

God's love reached its crescendo at Calvary with Christ's words of suffering forgiveness. Yes, the cross is the most complete and the most beautiful demonstration of divine love. The apostle Paul says it this way: "God proves his love for us in that while we were still sinners Christ died for us."† In Christ, God reveals that his disposition toward us is not one of vengeful retaliation but one of forgiving love. His nature of forgiving love is supremely demonstrated in Christ at the cross. When Jesus could have summoned twelve legions of avenging angels, he instead prayed for his enemies to be forgiven. Vengeance had been canceled in favor of love. Retaliation was overruled in favor of reconciliation. Payback had been abandoned in favor of forgiveness. This is beautiful, and it is the beauty that saves the world.

Beauty can be found in various forms, both artistic and natural. There is also a kind of beauty that can be found in

---

* 1 John 4:8, 16
† Romans 5:8, NRSV

human altruistic action. We recognize acts of compassion, acts of courage, and acts of sacrifice as beautiful. It is in compassion, courage, and sacrifice that we find the beauty of a saint. The compassion of Mother Teresa as she cared for the dying in Calcutta is esteemed as something beautiful. We view the courage of hundreds of firefighters running into burning towers to save others as a beautiful thing. The sacrifice of Oskar Schindler spending his fortune to save Jews from the Holocaust is honored as a beautiful act. And each of these saintly acts of beauty emerged in the midst of great ugliness. The beauty of Mother Teresa's compassion is set in the ugliness of Calcutta's dehumanizing poverty. The courage of New York firefighters rushing into the World Trade Center is set amidst the ugly horror of 9/11. The beauty of Oskar Schindler's sacrifice occurs in the ugliness of Nazi genocide.

But at the cross we find beauty in its fullest and finest form. In Christ we behold the beauty of unconditional compassion, supreme courage, and ultimate sacrifice. In fact, the beauty of Mother Teresa, Oskar Schindler, and New York City firefighters is a kind of reflection of the beauty that finds its ultimate form in Christ at Calvary. This is the beauty of the cruciform. It is the beauty of self-sacrifice. In the ugliest experience of human existence—death by crucifixion—God reveals himself in Christ as absolute, unconditional, self-giving love. At Calvary, all of the ugliness of the world—its greed and pride and lust and hate and cruelty and violence—is poured into Christ. And, upon the cross, Jesus turns all of this ugliness into the beauty of forgiving love. This is the greatest of miracles, and nothing is more beautiful!

Of course the beauty of the cross is seen only in retrospect of the Resurrection. Good Friday is not good until Easter Sunday. But with an Easter-informed perspective, we understand the beauty and supreme goodness of Good Friday. From a post-Resurrection vantage point, we understand that the action of Christ in forgiving his enemies on the cross was not foolish or delusional but the beauty that saves the world. The Resurrection is God's endorsement of forgiving love.

Through the Resurrection, God testifies that there can be a new beginning without the loss of history and identity. The Resurrection proclaims that forgiveness can save the sinner without erasing his history or obliterating his identity. Through the cross we come to see the final truth of forgiving love as the meaning of history. What is the purpose of history? What does God intend for us? Where are we headed? God intends for us to find forgiveness and practice forgiveness through faith in his crucified and resurrected Son. This is the way to peace. This is the way to beauty. It is in the way of forgiveness that we find beauty and become beautiful—and this is all accomplished through the paradox of the cross. The cross is an instrument of torture and execution that became a symbol of beauty and saving grace.

The Romans devised crucifixion to be the most hideous spectacle in the world. And it was. Crucifixion was a sight so ugly and so horrifying that the image would be permanently seared into the minds of all who ever witnessed a crucifixion. Multitudes were eyewitnesses of Roman crucifixions. Crucifixion was a public event and a common sight in the Roman world. It was the form of punishment inflicted upon rebels, revolutionaries, and renegade slaves—often en masse. It was the ghastly symbol of a brutal empire that used murder and terror as psychological weapons against all threats to its imperial interests. Crucifixion was not the most efficient way to carry out a death penalty, but it was deliberately designed to be ugly and repulsive, an effective deterrent to this sort of crime. The propaganda purpose of crucifixion was to cause any would-be rebel to think twice before challenging the supremacy of the Roman Empire.

Two thousand years ago it would have seemed utterly

inconceivable that a Roman cross would someday be an object of beauty, that it would be an icon of grace inspiring artistic creativity. The cross was anything but that. The Roman cross was the gallows, the guillotine, the electric chair, the lethal injection table of its day, except that it was infinitely more gruesome. That the Roman cross has become a symbol of faith, love, and beauty is utterly miraculous. How did this happen?

> *If the forgiveness of Christ can save a symbol from its ugly association with torture and death and transform it into a symbol of grace and beauty, then no sinner is beyond the reach and saving grace of God's love.*

The Roman cross itself was saved and redeemed because of what Christ did upon the cross. Instead of hurling curses and calling for revenge while he died on the cross, Jesus Christ forgave from the cross. That act of dying forgiveness—vindicated by the Resurrection—sealed the fate of the Roman cross. In time the cross would cease to be an ugly image of torture, psychological terror, and state-sponsored execution. Instead it would become the symbol of love. The symbol of forgiveness. The symbol of the Christian faith itself. The cross had been the symbol of the ugliest thing human beings can do—torture and kill—but because of its association with the forgiveness of Christ, it became a symbol of beauty.

Don't miss this miracle! The miracle of the redeemed Roman cross! Ugliness transformed into beauty. A miracle achieved not by erasing its history but by transforming its identity. The miracle of forgiving grace! And if the forgiveness of Christ can save a symbol from its ugly association with torture and death and transform it into a symbol of grace and beauty, then no sinner is beyond the reach and saving grace of God's love. The history of the cross is not obliterated through forgiveness—it retains its history of death—but the identity of the cross is transformed by forgiveness.

The same is true for the sinner. The forgiveness of the cross does not obliterate the history of the sinner but transforms the sinner. In the same way that the cross is transformed from an emblem of ugliness into an icon of beauty, so Christ's forgiving love transforms the sinner into a work of art. The prayer, "Oh, to be a work of art," is answered through the cross.

> *The Christian call is the call to cast away the ugliness of hate and retaliation and become beautiful icons of the love and forgiveness of Christ.*

Reject the Glamorous for the Truly Beautiful

Dostoevsky was right. It is beauty that saves the world. The beauty of unconditional love. The beauty of forgiving grace. The beauty of the cross. The beauty of cruciform love. The beauty of a Christlike love shaped by the cross. This is the beauty we are called to practice when we are invited by Jesus to take up our cross and follow him. We must understand the call to take up our cross and follow Jesus as first of all a call to the beauty of forgiveness—the beauty of forgoing retaliation for the practice of radical forgiveness. But this is too often forgotten or ignored. The call to take up the cross and follow Jesus is not a call to believe something about Jesus and his cross; it is the call to take up our own cross and *do* what Jesus did on his cross.

What did Jesus do on the cross? He forgave unconditionally. This is what it means to take up your cross and follow Jesus—to forgive unconditionally. When we reduce taking up the cross to adopting Christian doctrine alone, we deprive Christianity of its true beauty. And Christianity deprived of its true beauty can become downright ugly!

Religiously inspired intolerance can lead people to do extremely ugly things. Crusades and inquisitions are what happen when Christianity loses the beauty of imitating Christ. A Christianity that, though orthodox in doctrine, is retaliatory in attitude is a Christianity that has betrayed the cross and lost its beauty. A Christianity that is absent the beauty of imitating Christ in nonretaliatory, unconditional forgiveness becomes a Christianity focused on its own interests and self-preservation. This is the ugly Christianity that demands rights and angrily protests when it is treated by the world as Christ was treated by the world. The irony is tragic.

We are often tempted to glamorize retaliation. This is a forte of Hollywood. Hollywood knows how to make revenge look and feel glamorous. Hollywood makes lots of money doing it. But the glamour of vengeance is only a thin veneer covering a deep ugliness—the ugliness of hate and violence. The Christian call is the call to cast away the ugliness of hate and retaliation and become beautiful icons of the love and forgiveness of Christ. The deliberate intention to become a living icon of Christ is what produces the beauty of an apostle Paul, the beauty of a Saint Francis, the beauty of a William Wilberforce, the beauty of a Mother Teresa. Our lives become a work of art as we become living icons of Christ—as we become those who bear the beautiful image of Christ and his forgiving love in the midst of an ugly and vengeful world.

One of the primary challenges for the contemporary

Christian is to reject the glamorous for the truly beautiful. Our challenge is to reject a Hollywood movie poster-kind of obsession with the glamorous and sensational in favor of a kind of Christianity represented in the deep and sacred beauty of an icon. We are not called to be stars but saints. We are not called to produce a Christianity that looks like a Hollywood movie poster but a Christianity that looks like an icon. We are called to be icons in the sense that we are called to faithfully bear the beautiful image of Christ.

When we insist upon our own way, fight for our rights, and all too gleefully pronounce God's wrath upon our enemies, we fail to be a true icon of Christ. We are more like a glamorous "Christian" vigilante starring in a vengeance-themed movie. Rambos for Jesus. And no one (other than our own tribe) finds this beautiful. The inspiration we find in a Francis of Assisi or a Mother Teresa is that their lives were utterly lacking in glamour and absolutely filled with beauty. We cannot look at their lives without being reminded of Jesus Christ. In this way, they were true saints and beautiful icons of Christ.

Mark's Gospel tells us that when the Roman officer in charge of the crucifixion saw how Jesus died, he exclaimed, "Truly this man was the Son of God!"* What did this soldier see that led to this amazing confession? What was it about the way Jesus died that had such a profound effect on this Roman? Might it be that Jesus died loving and forgiving his enemies? The Roman centurion standing guard at the cross had undoubtedly witnessed many crucifixions. He knew how crucified men died— and they did not die with a prayer of love and forgiveness on their lips. This battle-hardened Roman soldier standing at the foot of a Roman cross instinctively recognized this kind of love as from another world. His only explanation was that this Nazarene being crucified for the crime of claiming to be the

---

* Mark 15:39

king of the Jews must be divine! It was the transcendence of forgiving love alone that could persuade a Roman soldier that a crucified Galilean Jew was the Son of God. This is the persuasion of love. Or as Hans Urs von Balthasar said, "Love alone is credible."[8]

This is the love we are called to follow; this is the love we are called to imitate—the cruciform love of radical forgiveness. No other apologetic argument will come close to the persuading power of cruciform love—a love that does not retaliate but offers unconditional forgiveness. If we can take up our crosses and follow Jesus in this practice, even our enemies will be found confessing, "Truly these are the sons and daughters of God." This is how the world will know we are the sons and daughters of God and the brothers and sisters of Jesus Christ. Whether we understand it or not, nonbelievers instinctively know it is by being Christlike that we are truly Christian. Didn't Jesus say we would be known for our love?* It's not by winning a debate, and much less by fighting for our rights or protesting the sins of our enemies, that we imitate Christ. It's by the practice of radical and unconditional forgiveness. By forgiving seventy times seven. By taking the ugliness of hate and turning it into the beauty of forgiveness. This alone is truly Christlike, and this alone is the beauty that saves the world.

Get On the Right Train

Western Christianity is at a critical juncture. We are like people who have taken a train to the end of the line. We are now at the terminus looking for the proper platform to catch the right train that will take us farther down the line to our intended destination. It can be a bit confusing. The reformation of five hundred years ago, though it brought necessary theological

---

* John 13:35

correction, also placed us on a trajectory to become angry protesters. The Protestant Reformation was an argument within Christendom. It was an argument among Christians about Christian doctrine and practice. But medieval Christianity is not the world we live in. We no longer live within a Christendom where Christianity is assumed. We live in the secular and increasingly skeptical Western world of the twenty-first century. Our challenges are not those of sixteenth-century Europe.

If we are going to persuade a skeptical and secular world of the beauty of Christ, we have to do so *on its terms*. Simply citing chapter and verse and shouting, "The Bible says," is going to be largely ineffective. Telling a secular world that Jesus is the way because John 14:6 says so is insufficient. We must persuade people that Jesus is the way by demonstrating the way as *living epistles*.

No other argument will be as persuasive as the beauty of cruciform love. Our credibility will be found in our love, not our protest. Protest has been our heritage. Protest is in our DNA. But the protest train has come to the end of the line. It's time we left the protest train to catch the cruciform train. Why? Because love alone is credible. When we become true disciples of the One who forgave from the cross, then the skeptics will confess that we are the sons and daughters of God.

You can stay on the protest train if you like, but that train has come to the end of the line, and it isn't going anywhere. I would like to invite you to join the cruciform train—a train that can carry Christianity into the twenty-first century in a compelling and engaging way.

This is the twenty-first-century reformation we need. A cruciform reformation. A cross-shaped re-formation of Christianity. No longer using *protest* as our dominant paradigm but returning to the cruciform to recover our true (and beautiful) shape. To do this we must carefully examine our doctrines, practices, and attitudes by holding them up to the true form of the crucified Savior. And if our doctrines, practices, and attitudes do not conform to the cruciform—to Christ upon the cross—then we need to either abandon them or re-form them according to the true form. This is how twenty-first-century Christianity can and must recover its beauty. This is the cross-shaped beauty that can save the world.

10

THE PRINCE OF PEACE

P EACE. PEACE AMONG nations. World peace. It's the wish of dippy beauty queens. It's also the dream of the prophets. In our war-torn world, it's easy to be cynical about any prospects for peace that go beyond the realm of our own private emotions. But the Bible does not endorse such cynicism. In one sense, peace has always been an impossible dream—but a dream the prophets dared to imagine anyway. The first mention of peace among the prophets is when the prophet Isaiah speaks of a Prince of Peace.

> For unto us a child is born,
>   to us a son is given;
> and the government shall be upon his shoulder,
>   and his name shall be called
> Wonderful Counselor, Mighty God,
>   Everlasting Father, Prince of Peace.
> Of the increase of his government and of peace
>   there will be no end.
> —ISAIAH 9:6–7

Ever since Cain rose up in the field against Abel, the world has not been a very peaceful place. Human history is written in blood and is largely the record of where, when, and why blood was spilled. But still the prophets dream. They dream of swords that become plowshares, and spears that become pruning hooks. In a modern world, they would dream of tanks becoming tractors and missile silos becoming grain silos. The cold, hard pragmatist will dismiss their dreams as utterly incongruent with the way the real world runs. But this is the role of the prophet—to give a minority report based upon prophetic imagination. In their wild, impractical, impossible, God-breathed poems they mount a challenge to the brutal tyranny of pragmatism. And I say, God bless them.

We need an alternative vision. We need a dream that isn't censored by the status quo. We need an imagination that transcends the dominant script. We need the poems of the prophets, because we live in a world where peace is treated as an unwelcome vagrant by those who have placed their faith in the game the way it has always been played.

> We live in a political world
> Where peace is not welcome at all,
> It's turned away from the door to wander some more
> Or put up against the wall.[1]

So instead of surrendering to the assumption that the world, as is, is the way it must be, the prophets fly in the face of convention and insist there must be a better way. The prophets are incapable of shrugging their shoulders at massive injustice and sighing *que sera, sera*. In a world where every day the nations spend three billion dollars on military defense while seventeen thousand children die of hunger,[2] the prophets will not embrace the status quo as either acceptable or inevitable. The prophets are the burr under the saddle of those committed to an intransigent paradigm.

During a time when the nation of Israel lived in the shadow of the ominous Assyrian Empire, the prophet Isaiah envisioned God's deliverance in the form of a child yet to be born—a child who would become a king and bear the responsibility of governance upon his shoulders and succeed where the rest had failed. He speaks of this child in the most superlative ways. The prophesied Son of David will give us wonderful counsel; he will be mighty God among us; he will be the progenitor of a new way of being human; he will be the Prince of Peace. It's the title *Prince of Peace* that we remember best of all, possibly because it resonates with our deepest longings. Messiah as the Prince of Peace is a favorite theme for Christmas carols and Christmas cards. But it's more than that—especially if you liberate the title from archaic language. Today we would speak of a president or a prime minister of peace. A governor ushering in a government of peace is how Isaiah and the rest of the prophets understood the kingdom of God—this kingdom would somehow be the government of God among us, and it would be the legitimate hope for peace.

A Government That Produces Peace

If the Hebrew prophets were daring in their dreams, the Christian apostles were even bolder in their speech. They not only endorsed the dream of the prophets—the dream that God would someday govern through a son whom he would give— but they also dared to announce that the government of the Son of God had actually begun! It is a government that produces peace. It is undeniable that peace is one of the prominent themes of the apostolic gospel. Paul and Peter and the rest of the apostles believed they were proclaiming something profoundly important pertaining to peace. Although the peace of Christ includes personal, inner peace, we must not so privatize the gospel as to make peace only a matter of private mental health. As the apostle Paul writes about the accomplishments of Christ concerning peace in his letter to the Ephesians, his primary emphasis is *not* a private inner peace but a peace between ethnic groups who have had a long history of bitter enmity.

> For he is our *peace*; in his flesh he has made both groups into one and has broken down the dividing wall, that is, the hostility between us. He has abolished the law with its commandments and ordinances, that he might create in himself one new humanity in place of the two, thus making *peace*, and might reconcile both groups to God in one body through the cross, thus putting to death that hostility through it. So he came and proclaimed *peace* to you who were far off and *peace* to those who were near.
> —EPHESIANS 2:14–17, NRSV, EMPHASIS ADDED

Paul says that Jesus is our peace, that he makes peace, that he proclaims peace, peace to those far and near. As modern Christians, when we talk about the peace of Christ, we instinctively limit our meaning to a private emotional state of well-being. For us, the peace of Christ is a psychological matter and not a political matter. We assume the peace of Christ pertains to the feelings of our inner world and has little to do with the geopolitical relations of the outer world. But our instincts are wrong. Our modern instincts create a division of public and private that is foreign to Scripture. And our modern, post-enlightenment prejudices show just how severely we have reduced the gospel. We have conspired with secularism to banish Christ to the realm of private religious concerns. In this division of

sacred and secular, Jesus is assigned to matters of private spiri-
tuality, while the matters of global and ethnic conflict are left to
those qualified to handle such matters—secular governments.
Such thinking is nothing less than a betrayal of the apostolic
gospel. L. Gregory Jones reminds us how vehemently Dietrich
Bonhoeffer rejected this approach to Christianity:

> If all that ultimately matters is individual autonomy,
> then forgiveness and reconciliation—which are
> designed to foster and maintain community—are of
> little importance.... These convictions led Bonhoeffer
> to polemicize against the trivialization and priva-
> tization of Christian life, and specifically Christian
> forgiveness.[3]

Christian forgiveness is not simply a private matter between
the sinner and God. Forgiveness has a horizontal dimension as
well. This is why in the Lord's Prayer we ask God to forgive us,
while in the same breath pledging to forgive others. Forgiveness
is God's way of achieving peace. In fact, it is ultimately the only
way of achieving peace between alienated parties. Justice alone
is incapable of producing peace. The peace the Bible is interested
in involves not only the cessation of hostilities but also the reconciliation of enemies. This is why Dietrich Bonhoeffer says:
"No peace is peace but that which comes through the forgiveness of sins."[4] This why the followers of Christ, who are both
the recipients and practitioners of radical forgiveness, should
be the leading authorities on peace. Of course we have to actually practice peace before we can be respected as authorities on
the subject. But this is what we are called to in Christ. This is
how we are to be the light of the world and the sons of God—
through a proclamation and practice of a gospel of peace based
in forgiveness.

If justice alone is incapable of producing peace, sheer might is even more incapable of producing peace. The peace of sheer might is the peace of propaganda. The Roman historian Tacitus records the Scottish chieftain Calgacus as wryly saying, "The Romans create a wilderness and call it peace."[5] Sheer might can create peace if all we mean by peace is the subjugation of dissent. But this is never what the prophets and apostles mean by peace. The prophetic and apostolic vision of peace is the peace of reconciliation and genuine harmony. This is the peace that forgiveness alone is capable of achieving. This is why Christians should have much to contribute to the subject of peace. In a world bereft of peace and drunk on hostility, Christians are called to be salt and light through the consistent practice of forgiveness-based peace.

Peace in All Dimensions

The mission of God is nothing less than the project to set right through the cross a world gone wrong through sin. Among our worst problems is our utter inability to live together in peace— especially when the enmity fostering hostility is between religions, ethnicities, and nations. It is this very enmity that the apostle Paul dares to say is overcome by the cross. Though the modern Christian may be cynical about peace and content to limit the achievement of the cross to "spiritual peace," Paul will have none of it. He believes that peace in every sense of the word is the full achievement of the cross:

> For in him all the fullness of God was pleased to dwell, and through him God was pleased to reconcile to himself all things, whether on earth or in heaven, by making peace through the blood of his cross.
> —COLOSSIANS 1:19–20, NRSV

The achievement of the cross is peace in all dimensions— on Earth and in heaven, spiritual and political, personal and global. If that peace is not yet fully seen—and it is not!—then we should regard it, not as an impossible task, but as a challenge to more faithfully take up the cross and follow Christ.

> *We are to be the light of the world and the sons of God—through a proclamation and practice of a gospel of peace based in forgiveness.*

Of course I am well aware of the supposed eschatological escape clause: "Sure, there will be peace when Jesus returns, but until then it's going to be wars and the road to Armageddon." Without challenging that eschatological interpretation, I will simply say that no theory of End Time events gives us license to rejoice in war or oppose peace. To put it bluntly: if the devil leads the nations of the world to war, we need not cheer him on.* Our theories of interpretation regarding the Book of Revelation cannot be used to exempt us from the clear teaching of Jesus found in the Sermon on the Mount. Jesus said, "Blessed are the peacemakers, for they shall be called sons of God."† No matter what End Time theory we subscribe to, we don't have the right to change Christ's beatitude to: "Suspicious are the peacemakers, for they probably work for the Antichrist." Jesus calls his disciples to love peace, proclaim peace, and work for peace at every possible level. So whether we work for peace within a family or among nations, we are engaged in the family business as the sons and daughters of God. Yes, wars do come, but they must not come in the name of Christ, and they should not be viewed as inevitable or assumed to be the will of God, and we are

---

* See Revelation 16:13–16.

† Matthew 5:9

certainly not enjoined to rejoice in them. As the apostle Paul says, "If possible, so far as it depends on you, live peaceably with all."* Or, as the apostle James says, "Peacemakers who sow in peace raise a harvest of righteousness."†

I remember being on the Mount of Olives in Jerusalem with two young brothers; they were zealous in their Christian faith, and their enthusiasm was infectious. For reasons that will become apparent, these teenagers reminded me of the brothers James and John whom Jesus nicknamed "the Sons of Thunder." As we were retracing Jesus's triumphal entry from the Mount of Olives into the city of Jerusalem, one of them exclaimed, "I can't wait for Jesus to come back so we can kick butt!" Kick-butt Christianity! The kind of Christianity where we let *them* have it! Unfortunately, that attitude is all too prevalent today, and it's the very attitude Jesus rebuked in the "Sons of Thunder" when they wanted to call down fire on the Samaritan village.‡ In response to the eagerness of my two young friends to "kick butt" with Jesus, I opened my Bible and showed them the passage from the prophet Zechariah that depicts a humble Messiah coming to Jerusalem riding a lowly donkey. This is a prophecy that Jesus knew and deliberately enacted when he requested a donkey for his entry into Jerusalem five days before his crucifixion.

> Rejoice greatly, O daughter of Zion!
>   Shout aloud, O daughter of Jerusalem!
> Behold, your king is coming to you;
>   righteous and having salvation is he,
> humble and mounted on a donkey,
>   on a colt, the foal of a donkey.
> I will cut off the chariot from Ephraim

---

* Romans 12:18
† James 3:18, NIV
‡ See Luke 9:51–56.

and the war horse from Jerusalem;
and the battle bow shall be cut off,
and he shall speak peace to the nations;
his rule shall be from sea to sea,
and from the River to the ends of the earth.
—ZECHARIAH 9:9–10

The two young zealots with me in Jerusalem were not the first to long for a "kick-butt" Messiah. This is exactly what the original Jewish revolutionary Zealots wanted. It's the vision of Messiah that Jesus steadfastly rejected. Instead of riding a warhorse into Jerusalem, as Pontius Pilate no doubt did, Jesus did something else. In a deliberate mockery of a Roman triumph (as a deliberate rejection of Roman ways), Jesus chose to ride a domesticated beast of burden instead of a warhorse. The warhorse was an obvious symbol of Roman imperial power—a symbol of both wealth and military might. In the first century B.C. there were many who wanted a Messiah who would do it the Roman way and beat the Romans at their own game—the game of kicking your enemy's butt. But Jesus had other plans. Jesus was choosing the way of humility, the way of salvation, the way of peace. So he chose the donkey. With his feet dragging the ground as he sat astride the little animal, the Roman soldiers, who had presumably seen a real triumph in Rome, must have had a good laugh at this peasant version of a triumph. The Galileans in their enthusiasm even dared to acclaim the donkey-riding carpenter from Galilee as the king of Israel. It must have all been terribly comical to the Roman sentries. Comical, because everyone knows a king rides a warhorse and not a donkey. But this king is different—this king is the Prince of Peace. And though the scoffing Romans could never have imagined it, the kingdom of this Prince of Peace has spread to the ends of the earth, just as Zechariah prophesied. Furthermore, the humble processional of this prince is commemorated all over the world every Palm Sunday. Yes, the Prince of Peace has established a global empire, and he did it all without kicking anyone's butt.

The Prince of Peace

But that doesn't mean the kingdom of God comes by nothing more than sweet words and well wishes. Jesus is the Prince of Peace whose crown was made of thorns, whose throne was a cross, whose acclamation was a mockery, whose triumph was a crucifixion, and whose kingdom was won by shedding his own blood. This prince calls his followers to take up their own crosses and follow him—which means nothing less than following his way of doing things. It's the way of the donkey, the towel, and the cross. The way of humility, service, and suffering. However we interpret the vision of the white-horse rider of Revelation with a sword in his mouth, the call here and now is to follow the Prince of Peace by taking up the cross of radical forgiveness. This is the way of peace. The question is: "Are we disappointed in a Christ who rejects the warhorse and chooses the donkey?" Can we accept a king who, in humility, speaks peace to the nations and in this way extends his rule from sea to sea? Can we accept the minority report of the Hebrew prophets?

The eighth century B.C. gave the world two great poets—the Greek Homer and the Hebrew Isaiah. These two poets offer competing visions of the heroic. Homer's epic poem *The Iliad* opens with this line: "Rage—Goddess, sing the rage of Peleus' son Achilles."[6]

But while Homer sings of the rage of Achilles, Isaiah sings of the peace of Immanuel. The question we face is which hero to embrace, Achilles or Immanuel? Whose vision will we allow to form us, Homer's or Isaiah's? Which way will we choose to follow, the rage of recompense or the peace of forgiveness? Throughout the centuries we've become quite comfortable with glorifying Achilles and his rage. But Achilles's way leads only to, as Homer says, "hurling down to the House of Death so many sturdy souls."[7] And though we love to lionize Achilles, I've never heard a Christmas carol that came from *The Iliad*. Isaiah is where George Frideric Handel found the inspiration for his timeless *Messiah*. As Christians we must follow Isaiah's suffering servant and John's slaughtered lamb and not try to turn Immanuel into a kind of Achilles. Achilles offers nothing more than the same old dead ends. It's in Immanuel that we find hope for the world.

A few years ago my wife and I were spending a week in Paris where I had been invited to speak in a church and teach in a Bible college. One evening I set out on my own to attend an event at Notre Dame Cathedral. It was a multimedia presentation dedicated to the history and construction of that magnificent achievement of medieval Gothic architecture. The date was October 8, 2004. I remember the date because it was the day Jacques Derrida died in Paris. Jacques Derrida was a famous French philosopher and the founder of deconstruction theory. His death was big news in Paris.

I took a train to Notre Dame and, arriving early, decided to visit the famous Shakespeare and Company bookshop located just across the river from the cathedral on the Left Bank. My thought was to pick up some reading material for the forty-five-minute train ride back to the hotel. As I wandered through the old bookshop, which had been the haunt of such literary elites as Ezra Pound, James Joyce, and Ernest Hemmingway, I found myself browsing among the Russian masters—Tolstoy, Dostoevsky, Chekhov, and so forth. I ended up buying a paperback copy of *The Idiot* by Fyodor Dostoevsky. The strange thing about my purchase was that I already had a nice hardback edition of *The Idiot* back at the hotel. It was the book I was currently reading. My rationalization was that I would be able to read forty-five more minutes of *The*

Idiot on the train ride back to the hotel. (I'll admit the idea seemed a bit extravagant to me at the time.) Having made my purchase, *The Idiot* and I headed back across the river to Notre Dame.

The presentation covered the nine-hundred-year history of the cathedral and opened with a brief biography of Saint Denis, the third-century Christian martyr who was beheaded for preaching the gospel in the year 275. I found the biographical account of this early Christian missionary very inspirational. At the conclusion of the presentation, I felt strangely moved, and as I sat by myself in the massive cathedral, I prayed a simple prayer: "God, use me more in Paris." Leaving the cathedral, I got on the train and started reading my new book. We had only gone one stop when a young Asian man got on the train and sat opposite me. I hadn't paid any attention to him until he said, "That's a great book you're reading."

I asked him if he'd read it, and he told me he was reading it right now, which we both thought was something of a coincidence. As we talked for the next few minutes, we discovered we had similar interests in philosophy and literature. We talked a little bit about Jacques Derrida, about Gabriel Garcia Marquez, and discovered we were both big fans of Fyodor Dostoevsky. His name was Yu, and he had just graduated from college with degrees in political science and history. I congratulated him on his graduation and told him he had chosen a good combination of degrees, because political science is the study of humanity's attempt to govern itself, and history is the record of humanity's failure in the attempt. He laughed and agreed.

Yu was obviously an intelligent young man, and I was curious about his worldview, so I asked him a question.

"You've just earned degrees in political science and history, both of which are disciplines that attempt to see the world in terms of the big picture. So what is your hope for the world?

Do you believe humanity has hope of achieving justice and producing peace?"

Yu was quiet for a moment and then said, "I have no such hope."

Then Yu asked me a question. "I've heard that Fyodor Dostoevsky was a Christian; do you know anything about that?"

At this point in the conversation I'm certain Yu didn't know I was a Christian, much less have any idea I was a pastor. But I was beginning to suspect that God was already answering my prayer to use me more in Paris.

So I told Yu the story of how at the age of twenty-seven, Fyodor Dostoevsky was arrested for belonging to a subversive intellectual group in Czarist Russia and was sentenced to death by firing squad. After being taken to the execution site, he was blindfolded and placed before the firing squad. Dramatically, at the very last moment, the sentence was commuted to five years hard labor in Siberia. Dostoevsky later said that he felt as though his life had suddenly been given back to him.

Upon arrival at the Siberian labor camp, a woman gave Dostoevsky a New Testament—the only book he would have for the next five years. During his prison years of acute suffering, Dostoevsky turned to the New Testament time and again and especially to the Gospel of John to find comfort. I've seen that well-worn Bible in the Dostoevsky museum in St. Petersburg. Like Aleksandr Solzhenitsyn a century later, it was during his prison years that Fyodor Dostoevsky came to have faith in Jesus Christ as the Savior of the world—a faith that would be expressed in his subsequent literary master-pieces in profound ways.

This is the story I told to Yu on the train in Paris. Yu seemed fascinated, and then asked me what I did and why I was in Paris. When I explained I was a pastor, he was initially surprised. Then he became serious, and leaning close to me, he said, "Since you are a pastor, I want to tell you something."

He went on to tell me that although he had grown up in a home that believed in God, when he was in his teen years he became an atheist and had been an atheist all through college. Then he leaned close to me and said, "Yesterday I went to Notre Dame, just to see the Gothic architecture. But the moment I walked into the cathedral I knew there is a God. I knew that I had been wrong. I tried to pray and tell God that I was sorry, but I don't think God heard my prayer because I walked away from him years ago."

I said, "Yu, let me tell you something. God *did* hear your prayer. Less than an hour ago, I was in that same cathedral, and I also prayed. I prayed, 'God, use me more in Paris.' Then I got on this train and you got on this train and we sat opposite from one another. And you commented on my book, which we are both reading, which I just bought, even though I already have a copy of it in my hotel room! All so we would meet and have this conversation and I could tell you that God most definitely heard your prayer in Notre Dame yesterday just as he heard my prayer tonight. God is answering both of our prayers!"

Yu was stunned, and tears were in his eyes.

Then I said to Yu, "Do you really want to know God? Do you want to know the hope for the world? The hope that I have found? The hope that Dostoevsky found? The hope for a world gone wrong? The hope for peace?"

"I do."

I asked Yu if he owned a Bible, and he said he did, but he hadn't read it.

"Yu, go home and read the Gospel of John like Dostoevsky did, and you will discover how to know God through Jesus Christ. You'll discover the hope for this world that can't be found anywhere else."

He assured me he would do this, and then I prayed for Yu right there on the train. When I said, "Amen," I looked up and

I was at my stop. I said, "Yu, I have to go," and I got off the train. I felt like an angel—an angel sent by God. I never learned Yu's last name or got any more information about him, but I'm confident that God used me in Paris on the day that Derrida died to help a young man find the Prince of Peace.

The Christian hope I testified to on the train in Paris is the Christian truth I testify to in this book. The truth that through the radical forgiveness of the cross, Jesus offers hope to the sinner and hope to the world. Hope on a personal level and hope on a global scale. Hope for reconciliation and hope for peace. And the hope for peace that I see is not a cheap panacea or the easily mocked beauty pageant wish. It is a peace that is both costly and possible– it is as costly as the cross and as possible as the kingdom of God.

The Hope for Peace

The hope for peace that I see is where sin is called sin and where the cross is seen as the solution. The hope for peace that I see is where lust for dominance is replaced by love and where lust for vengeance is replaced by forgiveness. The hope for peace that I see is the Jesus way of choosing the cross by refusing the deathtrap of recycled revenge. The hope for peace that I see is where the rage of Achilles is neither glorified as heroic nor satisfied in retaliation. The hope for peace that I see is where the rage of Achilles is named and shamed as the curse of Cain and extinguished at the cross. The hope for peace that I see is where the disciples of Jesus don't just watch in admiration as Jesus carries his cross, but practice an imitation of the same kind of cross-bearing forgiveness. This is the kind of Christianity that is not a chaplain to the status quo but can really change the world.

This is what we are praying for when we pray, "Thy kingdom come, Thy will be done." It is a prayer for God's government to come and God's policy to be done. On Earth—*now!*—as it is in heaven. It is a prayer for God's government of grace and God's policy of peace. It is a prayer for grace and peace to be accomplished for all and at every level through the cross of Christ. Not cheap grace or empty peace, but the grace and peace founded on forgiveness—a forgiveness that entered the world when the Son prayed upon the cross, "Father, forgive them," and the Father said, "Yes, my Son."

> *The hope for peace that I see is where the disciples of Jesus don't just watch in admiration as Jesus carries his cross, but practice an imitation of the same kind of cross-bearing forgiveness.*

This is the kingdom of God liberated from the diminutive world of private piety. This is the kingdom of God as the answer for all of the most serious problems facing our world—problems like political corruption, genocidal war, ethnic hatred, extreme poverty, egocentric leadership, environmental abuse, sexual abuse, devalued human life, pandemic disease, broken families, destructive addictions, crippling debt, spiritual emptiness, and every other systemic brokenness that prevents humans from being the image-bearing creatures God intended. The child has been born. The Son has been given. And for those who confess the death, burial, and resurrection of Jesus Christ, we expect—

> Of the increase of his government and of peace
> there will be no end,
> on the throne of David and over his kingdom,
> to establish it and to uphold it
> with justice and righteousness

from this time forth and forevermore.
The zeal of the LORD of hosts will do this.

—ISAIAH 9:7

This kingdom does not come by political machinations. This kingdom does not come by military might. It doesn't come by bullets or ballots, by elections or intrigues, by democracies or demagogueries. The kingdom of God comes quietly, almost secretly. Like seed growing, like bread rising. It comes like a long walk home. It comes in whispers and quiet conversations. It comes while people are sleeping. It comes in surprising ways and in unexpected places. It comes by unconventional means and by unauthorized agents. It comes through the gradual transformation of hearts and minds one life at a time. The kingdom of God comes in a million different ways as people become fascinated with Jesus Christ, find his forgiveness, and learn to extend it to others.

Where is this kingdom? Jesus said it is *among* you. This kingdom is seen and experienced among those who take seriously the call to be apprentices of the Jesus way. A way that calls us to forgive as we are forgiven, to forgive seventy times seven, to forgive the sins of others, to forgive the sins of enemies, to forgive unconditionally. This is the kingdom of God. It is radical—and it is the greatest thing ever! It is the hope for the world. I've never heard anyone describe it any better than Frederick Buechner:

> The Kingdom of God? Time after time Jesus tries to drum into our heads what he means by it. He heaps parable upon parable like a madman. He tries shouting it. He tries whispering it.... What he seems to be saying is that the Kingdom of God is the time...when it will no longer be humans in their lunacy who are in charge of the world but God in his mercy who will be in charge of the world. It's the time above all else

for wild rejoicing—like getting out of jail, like being cured of cancer, like finally, at long last, coming home. And *it is at hand*, Jesus says.[8]

If we can become convinced that the kingdom of God is real, that the kingdom of God is possible, that the kingdom of God is here, then we can finally find the courage to abandon our allegiance to the corrupt ideas of Adam and Achilles and Augustus. Ideas of rebellion, rage, and self-centered empire building. Ideas that have banished us from the garden, filled the house of the dead, and created wastelands cynically called "peace." If we can really be born again by a deep faith in Jesus and his way of radical forgiveness, we can at last see the kingdom of God. Instead of placing our faith in the *Pax Romana* or the *Pax Americana* we can at last place our faith in the *Pax Christus*.

> As followers of the Lamb, we must come to realize that it is only through the practice of radical forgiveness that we can achieve real peace. Peace with God comes by forgiving and being forgiven.

Perhaps you wonder if I have ever seen any signs of this coming kingdom of Christ with its reign of peace. I have. I have seen the kingdom of Christ in the form of a kiss. I saw it when a former Palestinian fighter and a former Israeli soldier stood in our church and embraced one another with a kiss. It was a holy kiss if there ever was one. My friends Taysir Abu Saada and Moran Rosenblit have met in Christ and formed an impossible friendship under the banner of the Prince of

Peace. Taysir had been a PLO sniper who fought with Yasser Arafat. Moran was an embittered Israeli soldier who had lost friends to a Palestinian terrorist attack. But in Christ they have become practitioners of unconditional love and radical forgiveness. The forming of their friendship wasn't easy and it didn't come cheap. Their friendship was formed, not by agreeing on everything, but by praying together. Today their common ground is not identical political opinions, but a common allegiance to Jesus Christ and his way of radical forgiveness. When I saw these two men abandon the tired script of hate and retaliation and embrace one another in a kiss of love and forgiveness, I saw the kingdom of Christ. And the healing that has happened between one Israeli and one Arab is the hope of healing for the world. The Israeli-Palestinian conflict is not something that can be solved by clichés. The same can be said for any deep, historic conflict. But as a Jewish follower of Messiah and an Arab worshiper of Isa (Jesus) have learned to imitate the Prince of Peace, they have found a forgiveness that transcends tragedy, a forgiveness that gives them a future, a forgiveness that can save a soul, a forgiveness that is the beauty that saves the world.

This is the possibility of forgiveness—the possibility of peace. It's not the false peace that comes from getting our way and triumphing over our enemies. It's the peace of Christ that comes by forgiving and being forgiven. It's the peace that comes through the triumph of love in the form of forgiveness. This is the peace Jesus achieved when he loved unconditionally and forgave from the cross. As followers of the Lamb, we must come to realize that it is only through the practice of radical forgiveness that we can achieve real peace. Peace with God comes by forgiving and being forgiven. We both receive forgiveness and extend forgiveness by faith. Forgiveness is nothing less than faith expressing itself

219

through love.* So as the people of faith, we keep on praying day by day, "Forgive us our debts as we forgive our debtors." We keep on forgiving seventy times seven. We keep on forgiving the sins of others and using the keys of the kingdom of heaven to liberate our world from the chains of hatred, which bind us to the cycle of revenge. This is how we follow our crucified and risen Lord. This is how peace comes to our heart, our home, our world. And peace doesn't come any other way. Indeed, no peace is peace but that which comes through the forgiveness of sins.

> Jesus said to them again, "Peace be with you. As the Father has sent me, even so I am sending you." And when he had said this, he breathed on them and said to them, "Receive the Holy Spirit. If you forgive the sins of anyone, they are forgiven them; if you withhold forgiveness from anyone, it is withheld."
> —JOHN 20:21–23

The Father sent Jesus on a mission of forgiveness—a mission that led Jesus to the cross. That Jesus was faithful in his mission and succeeded in opening the door to forgiveness and peace is the testimony of God in the Resurrection. Now Jesus sends us on the same mission—the mission of forgiveness. We too will have to take up the cross, because forgiveness is often a kind of suffering. But we believe that beyond the suffering of radical forgiveness lie the resurrection of love and the triumph of peace.

---

*   Galatians 5:6

NOTES

Chapter 1
The Question of Forgiveness

1. Simon Wiesenthal, *The Sunflower* (New York: Schocken, 1997), 14–15.

2. Ibid., 42–43.

3. Ibid., 54.

4. Ibid., 97–98.

5. Solomon Schimmel, *Wounds Not Healed by Time* (New York: Oxford University Press, 2002), 65.

6. "Reader's Digest." Words and music by Larry Norman. Copyright © 1973 (renewed 2001) GLENWOOD MUSIC CORP. and STRAW BED MUSIC. All rights controlled and administered by GLENWOOD MUSIC CORP. All rights reserved. International copyright secured. *Permission requested December 2012 of Hal Leonard Corporation.*

7. Dietrich Bonhoeffer, *The Cost of Discipleship* (New York: Touchstone, 1963, 1995), 90.

Chapter 2
The Possibility of Forgiveness

1. Jacob Neusner, *A Rabbi Talks With Jesus* (Montreal, Quebec: McGill-Queen's University Press, 2000), 68.

2. "Love Your Enemy" by Corrie ten Boom is reproduced with permission from *Guideposts* Magazine. Copyright © 1972 by *Guideposts*. All rights reserved.

3. Aleksandr Solzhenitsyn, *One Day in the Life of Ivan Denisovich* (Westport, CT: Praeger, 1963).

4. Aleksandr Solzhenitsyn, *The Gulag Archipelago*, Part IV: *The Soul and Barbed Wire* (New York: HarperCollins Publisher, 1974), "The Ascent," 611–613.

5. Nikolai Velimirović, "Prayer Regarding Critics and Enemies," viewed at http://www.brianmclaren.net/archives/prayer-regarding -critics-and-ene-1.html (accessed February 19, 2010).

Chapter 3
The Imitation of Christ

1. This event is recorded in the Jewish Apocryphal book of 1 Maccabees 2:67–68.

2. "Dark Eyes" by Bob Dylan. Copyright © 1985 Special Rider Music. All rights reserved. International copyright secured. Reprinted by permission.

3. "To Forgive" by Steve Taylor. Copyright © 1985, Birdwing Music (ASCAP) (admin. EMI CMG Publishing)/C. A. Music (ASCAP). All rights reserved. Permission requested December 2012.

4. "The Cross Is a Scandal" by Brian Zahnd.

5. Rachel Tulloch, "The Pain of Forgiveness," Ravi Zacharias International Ministries, October 1, 2009, http://dev.rzim.org/usa/ resources/read/asliceofinfinity/todaysslice.aspx?aid=10405 (accessed February 10, 2010).

6. Ibid.

7. CNN.com, "Betancourt to Larry King: FARC Captivity 'Was Hell,'" July 10, 2008, http://www.cnn.com/2008/WORLD/ americas/07/09/king.betancourt.intw/index.html (accessed February 10, 2010).

Chapter 4
No Future Without Forgiveness

1. Desmond Tutu, *No Future Without Forgiveness* (New York: Random House, Inc., 2000).

2. Statistic South Africa, "Statistical Release P0302: Mid-Year Population Estimates 2009," July 27, 2009, http://www.statssa.gov .za/publications/P0302/P03022009.pdf (accessed March 5, 2010).

3. Truth and Reconciliation Commission, "Amnesty Hearings and Decisions," http://www.justice.gov.za/trc/amntrans/index.htm (accessed March 5, 2010).

4. Tutu, *No Future Without Forgiveness*, 108.

5. Ibid., 54–55.

6. Friedrich Nietzsche, *Thus Spake Zarathustra* (New York: Cosimo, 2006), 95; originally published in 1911.

7. "Death and All His Friends." Words and music by Guy Berryman, Jon Buckland, Will Champion, and Chris Martin. Copyright © 2008 by Universal Music Publishing MGB Ltd. All rights in the United States and Canada administered by Universal Music – MBG Songs. International copyright secured. All rights reserved. *Permission requested December 2012 of Hal Leonard Corporation.*

8. Miroslav Volf, *Exclusion and Embrace* (Nashville, TN: Abingdon Press, 1996), 276.

Chapter 5
Forgiveness That Transcends Tragedy

1. Bonhoeffer, *The Cost of Discipleship*, 43–45.

2. Jack Nelson-Pallmeyer, *Jesus Against Christianity: Reclaiming the Missing Jesus* (Valley Forge, PA: Trinity Press, 2001), 188.

3. Brad Jersak and Michael Hardin, eds., *Stricken by God?* (Grand Rapids, MI: Wm. B. Eerdman's, 2007), 245.

4. Donald B. Kyrabill, Steven M. Nolt, and David L. Weaver-Zercher, *Amish Grace* (Hoboken, NJ: Jossey-Bass, 2007), xi.

5. Ibid., 25.

6. Ibid.

7. Ibid., 44.

8. Ibid., 45.

9. Ibid., 46.

10. Ibid.

11. Ibid., 49.

12. Ibid.

13. N. T. Wright, *Evil and the Justice of God* (Westmont, IL: Intervarsity Press, 2009).

14. Jersak and Hardin, eds., *Stricken by God?* 55.

15. Augustine, "Letter 133," in Philip Schaff, ed., *Nicene and Post-Nicene Fathers*, volume I, trans. by J. G. Cunningham (Buffalo, NY: Christian Literature Publishing Co., 1887), viewed at http://www.newadvent.org/fathers/1102133.htm (accessed February 26, 2010).

Chapter 6
Forgiveness and Justice

1. "One Too Many Mornings" by Bob Dylan. Copyright © 1964, 1966 by Warner Brothers, Inc.; renewed 1992, 1994 by Special Rider Music. All rights reserved. International copyright secured. Reprinted by permission.

2. Volf, *Exclusion and Embrace*, 215.

3. Ibid., 223.

4. Dietrich Bonhoeffer, *Life Together* (New York: Harper & Bros., 1954), 47, 45–46.

5. Reinhold Niebuhr and D. B. Robertson, *Love and Justice* (Louisville, KY: Westminster John Knox Press, 1957), 49.

6. Miroslav Volf, *The End of Memory* (Grand Rapids, MI: Wm. B. Eerdman's, 2006), 9.

Chapter 7
Killing the Hostility

1. John Donne, "Meditation No. 17: No Man Is an Island," *Devotions Upon Emergent Occasions*, http://isu.indstate.edu/ilnprof/ENG451/ISLAND/text.html (accessed February 26, 2010).

2. Jersak and Hardin, eds., *Stricken by God?* 373.

3. John Calvin, *Defensio Orthodoxae Fidei* (1554), 46–47, in John Marshall, *John Locke, Toleration and Early Enlightenment Culture* (New York: Cambridge University Press, 2010), 325.

4. John Steinbeck, *The Grapes of Wrath* (New York: Penguin, 2002), 341.

5. "Desolation Row" by Bob Dylan, copyright © 1965 by Warner Brothers, Inc.; renewed 1993 by Special Rider Music. All rights reserved. International copyright secured. Reprinted by permission.

6. Volf, *Exclusion and Embrace*, 154.

Chapter 8
The Golden Rule and the Narrow Gate

1. Saint Athanasius, *On the Incarnation* (Crestwood, NY: St. Vladimer's Seminary Press, 1993), 41–42.

2. Volf, *Exclusion and Embrace*, 24.

3. Jersak and Hardin, eds., *Stricken by God?* 245.

4. Bonhoeffer, *The Cost of Discipleship*, 190.

Chapter 9
Beauty Will Save the World

1. "Philosophia." Written by Kevin Gerard May and Michael Lynch. Copyright © 2009 ROGUES WRITER'S CIRCLE (ASCAP)/ Administered by BUGHOUSE (ASCAP). All rights reserved. *Permission requested December 2012 of Hal Leonard Corporation.*

2. Fyodor Dostoevsky, *The Brothers Karamazov* (Garden City, NY: Literary Guild of America, 1953).

3. Fyodor Dostoevsky, *The Idiot* (New York: Oxford University Press, 1868, 2008).

4. Aleksandr Solzhenitsyn, "Nobel Lecture in Literature, 1970," NobelPrize.org, http://nobelprize.org/nobel_prizes/literature/ laureates/1970/solzhenitsyn-lecture.html (accessed February 18, 2010).

5. Etty Hillesum, *Etty: The Letters and Diaries of Etty Hillesum 1941–1943* (Grand Rapids, MI: Wm. B. Eerdsman Publishing Co., 2002), 640, 545, 460, 491.

6. Abraham Joshua Heschel, *The Prophets* (Peabody, MA: Hendrickson's Publishers, 2007), 270.

7. Hans Urs von Balthasar, *Love Alone Is Credible* (San Francisco, CA: Ignatius Press, 2005).

8. Ibid.

Chapter 10
The Prince of Peace

1. "Political World" by Bob Dylan, copyright © 1989 by Special Rider Music. All rights reserved. International copyright secured. Reprinted by permission.

2. Anup Shah, "World Military Spending," GlobalIssues. org, September 13, 2009, http://www.globalissues.org/article/75/ world-military-spending#WorldMilitarySpending (accessed March 5, 2010); CNN.com, "U.N. Chief: Hunger Kills 17,000 Kids Daily," November 17, 2009, http://www.cnn.com/2009/WORLD/ europe/11/17/italy.food.summit/index.html (accessed March 5, 2010).

3. L. Gregory Jones, *Embodying Forgiveness* (Grand Rapids, MI: Wm. B. Eerdman's, 1995), 13, 37.

4. Bonhoeffer, *The Cost of Discipleship.*

5. Cornelius Tacitus, *The Agricola and The Germania* (Stilwell, KS: Digireads.com Publishing, 2008), 21–22.

6. Homer, *The Iliad*, trans. Robert Fagles (New York: Penguin, 1990), 77.

7. Ibid.

8. Frederick Buechner, *Secrets in the Dark* (New York: Harper-One, 2007), 157, emphasis added.

WHAT DO YOU DO ON THE WORST DAY OF YOUR LIFE?

Foreword by JENTEZEN FRANKLIN

?

WHAT TO DO
on the
WORST DAY
OF YOUR LIFE

BRIAN ZAHND

978-1-59979-726-7 / US $14.99

"My wife and I have read and reread every word in this book. It was like God's voice to us in one of the toughest seasons of our lives."

—JENTEZEN FRANKLIN
New York Times best-selling author of *Fasting*

The life of King David gives us a timeless model for how to experience God's restorative power in the midst of deep tragedy. Discover the steps you can take to recover from all life's challenges.

FREE NEWSLETTERS
TO HELP EMPOWER YOUR LIFE

Why subscribe today?

☐ **DELIVERED DIRECTLY TO YOU.** All you have to do is open your inbox and read.

☐ **EXCLUSIVE CONTENT.** We cover the news overlooked by the mainstream press.

☐ **STAY CURRENT.** Find the latest court rulings, revivals, and cultural trends.

☐ **UPDATE OTHERS.** Easy to forward to friends and family with the click of your mouse.

CHOOSE THE E-NEWSLETTER THAT INTERESTS YOU MOST:

- Christian news
- Daily devotionals
- Spiritual empowerment
- And much, much more

SIGN UP AT: **http://freenewsletters.charismamag.com**

8178